NATIONAL TRAIL GUIDES

CLEVELAND WAY

Ian Sampson

Photographs by Ian Carstairs

AURUM PRESS

The Countryside Agency

DEDICATION

To the memory of Richard Bell, the first Warden in the North York Moors
National Park, who generously shared his deep knowledge of the countryside
and the North York Moors in particular.

ACKNOWLEDGEMENTS

The author wishes to acknowledge the helpful advice and assistance provided
by the Rangers and Information Service of the North York Moors National Park.

Ian Sampson lives in Helmsley at the start of the Cleveland Way. For 16 years
he was an official of the North York Moors National Park.

This revised edition first published 2003 by Aurum Press Ltd in association
with the Countryside Agency

Book design by Robert Updegraff
Cover photograph: Roseberry Topping from Easby Moor
Title-page photograph: Robin Hood's Bay

Typeset by Wyvern 21 Ltd, Bristol
Printed and bound in Italy by Printer Trento Srl

CONTENTS

Circular walks appear on pages 29, 31, 48 and 124

How to use this guide

This guide to the 108-mile (175-kilometre) Cleveland Way is in three parts:

- The introduction, with an historical background to the area and advice for walkers.
- The path itself, split into nine chapters, with maps opposite the description for each route section. The distances noted with each chapter represent the total walking length of the Cleveland Way, including sections through towns and villages. This part of the guide also includes information on places of interest as well as a number of short walks which can be taken around each part of the path. Key sites are numbered both in the text and on the maps to make it easier to follow the route description.
- The last part includes useful information such as local transport, accommodation and organisations involved with the Cleveland Way.

The maps have been prepared by the Ordnance Survey® for this Trail guide using 1:25 000 Pathfinder® or Outdoor Leisure™ maps as a base. The line of the Cleveland Way is shown in yellow, with the status of each section of the Trail – footpath or bridleway, for example – shown in green underneath (see key on inside front cover). These rights of way markings also indicate the precise alignment of the Cleveland Way, which walkers should follow. In some cases, the yellow line on these maps may show a route that is different from that shown on older maps; walkers are recommended to follow the yellow route in this guide, which will be the route that is waymarked with the distinctive acorn symbol ♀ used for all National Trails. Any parts of the Cleveland Way that may be difficult to follow on the ground are clearly highlighted in the route description, and important points to watch for are marked with letters in each chapter, both in the text and on the maps. *Some maps start on a right-hand page and continue on the left-hand page – black arrows (➤) at the edge of the maps indicate the start point.*

Should there be a need to divert the Cleveland Way from the route shown in this guide, for maintenance work or because the route has had to be changed, walkers are advised to follow any waymarks or signs along the path.

KEY MAP 2

Distance checklist

This list will assist you in calculating the distances between your proposed overnight accommodation and in checking your progress along the walk.

location	approx. distance from previous location	
	miles	km
Helmsley	0	0
Rievaulx Bridge	2.8	4.5
Cold Kirby	2.9	4.7
White Horse	3.1	5.0
Sutton Bank	1.4	2.3
Sneck Yate	3.4	5.5
Black Hambleton	5.2	8.4
Osmotherley	2.8	4.5
Scarth Nick	2.9	4.7
Carlton Bank	4.3	6.9
Clay Bank	3.9	6.3
Bloworth Crossing	3.2	5.1
Kildale	6.0	9.7
Roseberry Topping	4.3	6.9
Slapewath	6.0	9.7
Skelton	2.5	4.0
Saltburn	1.9	3.1
Skinningrove	3.9	6.3
Staithes	4.9	7.9
Runswick	3.4	5.5
Sandsend	5.1	8.2
Whitby	3.1	5.0
Robin Hood's Bay	7.0	11.3
Ravenscar	3.4	5.5
Scarborough (Corner) (North Bay)	10.2	16.4
Scarborough (Spa)	2.3	3.7
Cayton Bay	2.9	4.7
Filey Brigg	4.4	7.1

PREFACE

The Cleveland Way is a beautiful path, full of variety and interest. It starts on the edge of the North York Moors National Park and follows the Cleveland Hills through the Park to the coast at Saltburn-by-the-Sea. From here, it follows the North Yorkshire and Cleveland Heritage Coast to Filey. Its unique combination of moorland and coastal scenery makes this one of our most popular National Trails. Circular walks inland make the path attractive to day visitors as well as to the seasoned long-distance walker.

Local authorities work with organisations such as the National Trust to maintain the path using Countryside Agency funding. The exposed nature of the path and its popularity make this a major task in some areas. The path is waymarked with a distinctive acorn symbol which signals that you are on the right route.

I hope you will enjoy using this book during many hours of walking on this delightful stretch of England's coastline.

Ewen Cameron
Chairman
Countryside Agency

PART ONE

INTRODUCTION

The highest point on the eastern seaboard of England lies at Boulby where the cliff line above Rock Cliff stands 666 feet (203 metres) above sea level. Walking southwards from this high point you look down on one of the many memorable coastal views along the Cleveland Way. A limitless world of sea and land is broken only by the first tempting glimpse of old Staithes, poking its nose in the air from a sheltered break in the cliffs. The outstanding scenic beauty of this coastline was acclaimed in 1974 when it was defined as a Heritage Coast by the Countryside Commission. Panoramic views are the keynote of the Cleveland Way along the 108 miles (175 km) of its horseshoe-shaped route around the edge of the North York Moors. This is an area of magnificent moorland, dale and coastal scenery which was designated as a National Park in 1952 and richly deserves the strongest measure of protection afforded to our heritage of beautiful countryside. For the most part the National Trail keeps to the highest points of the moorland escarpment, from Sutton Bank to Guisborough in the west, and accompanies the cliffed coastline in the east from Saltburn to Filey.

The Cleveland Way story

The North York Moors presents a fairly easily defined geographical area. Its physical boundaries are most dramatic on its western and eastern edges. The steep moorland escarpment overlooking the Vale of York and the rugged coastal cliffs set against the North Sea have provided useful lines of communications since prehistoric times.

Early impetus was given to the idea of a long-distance path after the founding of the Youth Hostels Association (England and Wales) in 1930, when the Middlesbrough Rambling Club supported the idea of a holiday walk with the provision of hostels along the route. Some 20 years went by before the National Parks Commission (now the Countryside Agency) gave official sanction to a long-distance 'Moors and Coast Path'. The length of the trail was matched by the time it took to complete the necessary negotiations and legal designation of public access along the route. After nearly 16 years of work the Cleveland Way was finally completed in 1969 and the official opening was performed at Helmsley Youth Hostel in May of that year.

Cleveland Way Project

The Cleveland Way Project was formed in 1989 and is a partnership between the Countryside Agency and the managing authorities of the North York Moors National Park, Redcar & Cleveland Borough Council and Scarborough Borough Council. Its main aim is to ensure that the route provides a high quality of experience for users, whilst protecting the landscape and wildlife of the path and its immediate surroundings.

The project has, most significantly, been involved with a major restoration programme along the popular moorland lengths of the Cleveland Way. These have suffered from heavy erosion in recent years, especially along those parts of the route that coincide with the Coast to Coast and the Lyke Wake Walk. Approximately 9 miles (14.5 km) of the Cleveland Way has been surfaced. Traditional path-building techniques, that fit attractively into the surrounding landscape, have been used. These include the use of stone slabs and the age-old method of stone pitching.

Footpath restoration is also necessary along the coastal section of the Cleveland Way due to the continual problem of coastal erosion.

The North York Moors National Park

The 20th century has brought the world's attention as never before to the natural environment and more particularly to the ever-increasing destruction of its dwindling natural resources, wildlife habitats and landscape beauty. On a global scale, champions of the cause have good reason to be disheartened. Conservation of the landscape in England and Wales took a major step forward in the 1950s with the designation of ten national parks. The North York Moors National Park covers an area of 554 square miles (1,435 square km).

The countryside reveals its best-kept secrets only to those who are prepared to take to their own two feet and travel beyond the tarmac road. The good news is that there are 1,400 miles (2,250 km) of public paths on the North York Moors along which you can explore one of the finest landscapes in England and Wales.

Geology

A glance at the ground beneath your feet will reveal a change in geology as you walk the length of the Cleveland Way. The well-drained limestones of the Tabular Hills give rise to short, springy turf along the escarpment edge north from Sutton Bank. The heartland of the Moors is formed by a massive block of acid sandstones and shales. The sandstone becomes obvious in sections where the nutrient-starved soils are denuded to expose a sandy-orange pathway streaking along the high edge of the Cleveland Hills. The need for caution along the coast path is occasioned not only by the steep cliffs but also by the unstable and slippery shales and boulder clay.

The picturesque cottages and solid Yorkshire farmhouses are constructed from the various limestones and sandstones quarried in the area. The geology is also in evidence through the centuries of mining and quarrying for alum, jet and ironstone. Although the scars of past industries are largely overgrown, the massive shale waste tips will not be missed along the route of the trail.

With one exception (a volcanic intrusion) all the rocks of the North York Moors were formed from sediments deposited in the seas and river deltas over 150 million years ago in the Jurassic period. The North York Moors is a classic area for a study of the Jurassic, and the deepest exposure of the beds lies in the cliffs from Robin Hood's Bay to Ravenscar.

Wildlife

As the largest area of moorland in England, the North York Moors is dominated by a single plant – heather. Each year this sombre backcloth is transformed in late summer when the heather bursts into bloom and a haze of purple covers the view. There are three different species of heather but by far the commonest is Scotch heather, or ling as it is often called, which comes into flower from August to late September. Earlier, in July, the deep purple flowers of bell heather and the lighter pink flowers of the cross-leaved heath occur in smaller patches. The red grouse and the meadow pipit are the two most obvious resident birds of the moor. Due to its size, whirring flight and obvious call – 'ge'back, ge'back' – the grouse will become familiar along the moorland section of the walk. Spring sees the arrival of the curlew, lapwing and golden plover to find nesting sites on the open moor.

For centuries there have been mines and quarries in the area. Boulby Potash Mine has the deepest mining shaft in England.

Woodlands and waysides exhibit their most colourful displays of wild flowers in spring. Bluebells and wood anemones appear before the trees are clothed in leaves, and primroses thrive on the coastal clays. Scurvy-grass, one of the few truly maritime plants seen along the coast, is a constant companion along the clifftop edge. This plant, with its flat-topped cluster of white flowers and rounded kidney-shaped leaves, was once eaten by sailors to avoid the vitamin-deficiency disease of scurvy, hence its name. More obvious companions on the coastal section will be the seabirds: the raucous calls of the larger gulls cannot be silenced. The majestic flight of the fulmar is worthy of a few moments' admiration.

Farming

We tend to look upon the heather moorland as the natural vegetation of an upland plateau untouched by human hand. We are deceived. This is no natural environment, it is a monoculture which began with the first tentative destruction of a mixed deciduous woodland by Stone Age people some 10,000 years ago. The forest cover was totally destroyed and the soils depleted by the Bronze Age farmers (2000 BC – 500 BC) who finally abandoned their exhausted plateau farmland, which became heath and moor.

Walking along the moorland escarpment you will be aware from time to time of the black-faced sheep grazing on the heather. Sheep farming on the Moors follows a tradition begun 800 years ago by the monks of Rievaulx who operated the first large-scale sheep enterprises on the North York Moors. There are some valuable breeding flocks among the 50,000 sheep which graze the open moor.

Richer farmland exists in the dales, the limestone plateaux of the Tabular Hills and the clay-covered coastal belt. Arable crops are grown on the limestone plateaux and along the coast but the predominant activity is livestock farming with the rearing and fattening of animals as well as dairying.

History

Twentieth-century changes did come to the North York Moors, though at a slower pace and less severely than in many places. The area has been cushioned in the past by its remoteness and more recently by its productive designation as a national park. There is still a sense of history in its villages, countryside and way of life. The evidence of history as far back as the settlement of the Moors by prehistoric people has been saved from obliteration largely by the area's remoteness, altitude and landowning interests in sheep and grouse. The Cleveland Way is never far from tangible clues of a former age. There is a rich assortment, including Stone and Bronze Age burial sites, Iron Age forts, Roman signal stations, Norman abbeys and castles, industrial scars from the 17th to 20th centuries, and picturesque cottages dating back over the last 200 years. You do not have to be a great student of history to find that occasionally you are transported in thought to a bygone age.

Planning your walk

What starts as an idea usually comes to fruition only after a bit of thinking and planning. The better the plan, the better the result and that applies equally to the enjoyment of completing a National Trail such as the Cleveland Way. This guidebook will take some of the heartache out of the task, so start planning now.

There are 108 miles (175 km) to walk between the starting point at Helmsley and the official finish of the Cleveland Way on Filey Brigg. From this rocky promontory the walk into Filey will add a further 1½ miles (2.4 km).

An early task will be to divide the total distance into what you personally regard as suitable daily sections. The sections given in this guide can all be achieved individually within a day's walking. Some sections, however, are quite tiring and you may wish to shorten them. Total flexibility is just not possible, because there are constraints on the availability of accommodation *en route* and on interconnecting public transport services to the nearest town or village (see 'Useful Information'). At this stage the constituent parts of the jigsaw puzzle are accommodation, transport, your own walking pace and any time-consuming gradients or hindrances. As a rough estimate, an average walking rate is 2 miles (3.2 km) per hour, but it is best to allow an hour either side when calculating your daily mileage target. Any difficult sections are indicated at the beginning of each chapter to help with your planning.

Unless you are especially determined, it would be wise to plan for a minimum of eight days' walking to complete the Cleveland Way. There is a wide range of interesting places to visit *en route* and a few extra days will be well justified.

Waymarking

The route of the Cleveland Way is signposted at most junctions with other paths or roads. The signposts bear the words 'Cleveland Way' and the Countryside Agency's National Trail symbol – a stylised acorn. Elsewhere along the Trail, the acorn waymarker provides confirmation of the route.

Weather

The Cleveland Way has the distinct advantage of being on the east coast – the driest part of England. However, local peculiarities can sometimes cause severe weather conditions along the route. The steep moorland escarpment takes the full force of the prevailing westerlies racing straight across the Vale of York. The coastal section also endures a chilling effect whenever the polar air stream moves in from the north-east. A sea-fret, known locally as a 'roak', is a notorious feature of the summer. A low blanket of fog envelopes the coast and is accompanied by a slowly penetrating drizzle.

A pre-recorded weather forecast for north-east England is available 24 hours a day on 09068 505318. Weather forecasts are a useful guide but you should be prepared for unexpected and sudden changes.

The pier at Saltburn, where the moorland walk becomes coastal.

Safety precautions

Good planning will make for a safe, enjoyable walk. Check that you have set yourself a reasonable daily mileage target, have adequate clothing and emergency equipment (see page 140).

Take particular care when walking the coastal section of the Cleveland Way. The cliffs are steep, liable to occasional slumping and the clifftop path can be slippery in wet weather. Do not walk along the shoreline (except where indicated in the guidebook) – an 'escape' route from an incoming tide cannot be guaranteed.

The Cleveland Way is never more than a few miles from a tarmac road. Nevertheless, in conditions of deteriorating visibility you should check your map and compass for an appropriate 'escape' route from the Way.

In an emergency, check the location of the nearest farm, village or country telephone box. The person going for help should take this guidebook: its maps provide a means of locating your position. Telephone the police (tel. 999) who will give advice and arrange for a rescue team if necessary.

In the worst situation you may need to make the International Distress Signal with a torch or whistle (six long flashes or blasts in quick succession, repeated at one-minute intervals).

PART TWO

CLEVELAND
WAY

The gaunt ruins of Helmsley Castle, besieged by Parliamentary troops during the Civil War in 1644.

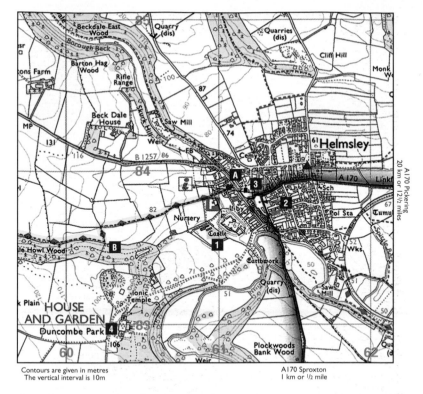

Contours are given in metres
The vertical interval is 10m

A170 Sproxton
1 km or ½ mile

1 Helmsley to Sutton Bank

past Rievaulx Abbey and the White Horse of Kilburn
10¼ miles (16.5 km)

The first section of the Cleveland Way provides an easy walk
across the richly wooded landscape of the Rye Valley, then rises
gently to the flat limestone plateaux of the Tabular Hills. At the
end of this section there is a spectacular view from the escarpment edge between the White Horse and Sutton Bank.

   The start of the Cleveland Way is the old market cross in
Helmsley's Market Square. Leave the Market Square by the
north-west corner, which leads you past the lych gate entrance
to All Saints' Church **3**.

   Turn right along the Stokesley road (B1257) for 100 yards (90
metres) then left **A** along the road signposted 'Footpath to
Rievaulx', opposite the Feversham Arms Hotel. Continue on
this road to the car park entrance near which you will find a
sculptured stone with a large acorn. The names chiselled out
on the base rocks are those of places along the Cleveland Way.

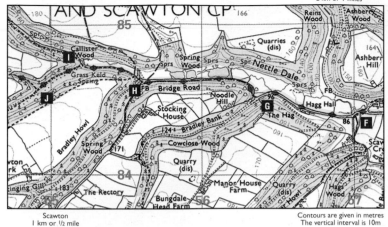

Scawton
1 km or ½ mile

Contours are given in metres
The vertical interval is 10m

Helmsley Castle **1** comes into view as you continue straight ahead, past the car park and along the rough stony track. The track continues along the edge of two fields. At the end of the track, go through the hand gate and turn left to follow the enclosed path down to the woodland.

At the woodland, turn right and walk alongside the woodland **B**, walking westward. The route continues along the enclosed path and then you turn left, through a gateway, to descend the steps into the steep little valley of Blackdale Howl (*see map on page 23, continuing opposite*). Steps lead out of the valley at the other side, where you follow the path with a wire fence on your left. Alongside the path are concrete bases marking the site of an army camp built here during the Second World War.

Continue straight ahead **C** after leaving the wooded area with a delightful small lodge on your right. Your reward at the top of Jinny York Bank is a magnificent view down into the flat alluvial valley of the meandering River Rye and across to Scawton Moor.

Keeping the lodge on your right, walk westwards along the field edge with the plantation on your left. The route leads into the plantation and descends the hillside to meet the Helmsley to Rievaulx road **D**. Turn left along the roadside path.

The ruined remains of the 12th-century Rievaulx Abbey **5** come into view across the fields on your right. Just before Rievaulx Bridge you have an opportunity to turn right **E** and make a 1-mile (1.6-km) return detour to visit the abbey. Any enthusiast of ancient buildings should allow an hour to view what many consider to be one of the most beautiful abbeys in England.

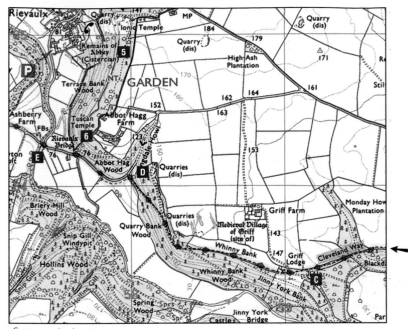

Contours are given in metres
The vertical interval is 10m

Cross the River Rye by Rievaulx Bridge **6**. This hump-backed stone bridge was rebuilt in the middle of the 18th century, the previous one having been destroyed in the flood of 1754.

Continue along the road. At the junction **F** continue ahead (do not take the Cold Kirby–Old Byland road). Notice the attractive setting of the whitewashed Ashberry Farm with its backcloth of trees surrounding Ashberry Hill and fronting on to Nettle Dale beck.

You pass two houses on your left and further on you leave the road after the bend **G** and take a right turn through a gate giving access to a forestry track which sweeps round Noodle Hill. The track soon follows the stream in Nettle Dale, where you will see some artificial lakes created to attract wildfowl.

Leave the track to take the stepping stones on your right over the beck, close to where it emerges as a spring. Go through a gate (often muddy underfoot) to join the forestry track **H** straight ahead up Nettle Dale. At the junction of two forest tracks **I** turn left up the dry valley of Flassen Dale (do not follow the right-hand bend of the main track). A short distance along here, at a break in the forest, turn right and climb steeply up a side gully **J**. On reaching the grass field

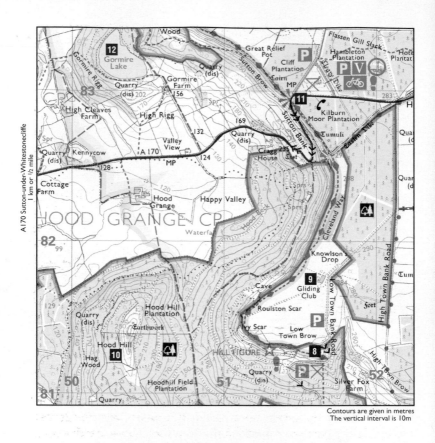

Contours are given in metres
The vertical interval is 10m

continue ahead with the field fence on your left. There are wide
views here across the flat tops of the Hambleton Hills. The path
joins Low Field Lane which rises gently in a long straight line
towards Cold Kirby (*see map on page 27, continuing above*). Low
Field Lane takes a left bend; turn right here **K** down a short
slope and then swing left up into Cold Kirby, whose name you
will appreciate if you experience a fresh north-easterly at this
exposed site 800 feet (245 metres) above sea level.

Walk through the village. Immediately past the last house on
the left, turn left along the pleasant lane called Cote Moor Road
L. The walled lane turns right then left, southwards along the
field edge to reach a forestry track **M**. Turn right and continue
walking westwards along the track.

At the end of this section of forest **N** continue straight ahead
over the stile. Follow the fenced path, with Hambleton House
on your right, to reach the driveway. The fine area of open
downland **7** is still used for training racehorses.

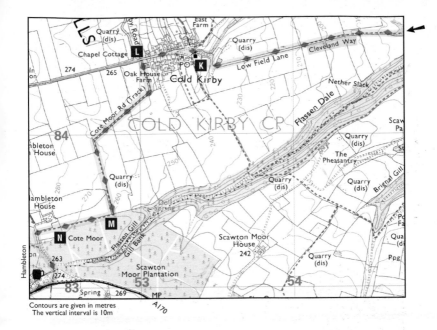

Contours are given in metres
The vertical interval is 10m

Cross the stile and turn left along the driveway to reach the A170 at the Hambleton Hotel which offers refreshments. Turn right along the main road until you reach the junction for Kilburn and the Yorkshire Gliding Club. Cross the road **O** and take the track, bisecting the angle of the roads, into the forest alongside the earthworks called Casten Dike. These earthworks are an enigma; even archaeologists do not know when they were constructed or for what purpose.

The forest ride ends at the steep escarpment edge of the Hambleton Hills. This gives a fine vantage point from which to view the glorious panorama over the Vale of York stretching westward to the Yorkshire Dales. Once again the landscape provides a generous reward towards the end of this first section of the Cleveland Way.

From this point on the escarpment edge there is the first official detour along the Trail. The White Horse of Kilburn **8** is just a mile (1.6 km) south along the path around the edge of Roulston Scar. The 300-foot (90-metre) long White Horse is a well-known landmark visible to the naked eye from many miles around. You can see it from York (the Minster tower) and Harrogate.

The round tower of the Yorkshire Gliding Club **9** is seen rising above the table-top grassland. You will be in line with the

Scale approx 2 inches to 1 mile

Contours are given in metres
The vertical interval is 10m

runways as you walk towards Roulston Scar with its warm creamy-coloured gritstone face. The distinctive knoll of Hood Hill **10** is just a giant's leap from the edge here.

From the White Horse retrace your steps and continue along the escarpment edge to reach the A170 and Sutton Bank.

On the escarpment edge at Sutton Bank **11** there is a view indicator which locates the features of interest across the panorama. The Trail crosses the main A170 from Thirsk to Helmsley. Here at the top of Sutton Bank is a visitors' centre with shop, tearoom, toilets and car parks provided by the National Park Authority.

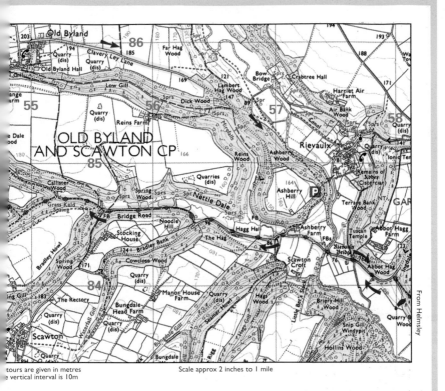

From Helmsley

tours are given in metres
e vertical interval is 10m

Scale approx 2 inches to 1 mile

A CIRCULAR WALK BETWEEN HELMSLEY AND SUTTON BANK

16 miles (26 km) (see maps on pages 23, 25 and above)

This walk uses the Cleveland Way to reach Sutton Bank. The return route via Cold Kirby and Old Byland mainly uses pleasant country roads.

Start from Helmsley Market Place and follow the Cleveland Way to the Hambleton Inn (see pages 23 to top of 27 for route description). On reaching the A170 at Hambleton, turn right and follow the roadside edge to Sutton Bank car park (this omits the route to the White Horse). Turn right into the car park and walk past the Sutton Bank Visitor Centre through to the northern end of the car park.

Turn right on reaching the Cold Kirby road. Follow the road route signposted through the village of Cold Kirby and Old Byland back to Rievaulx Bridge. From there retrace your steps back to Helmsley.

This walk can easily be shortened by 5 miles (8 km) if you start and finish at Rievaulx village.

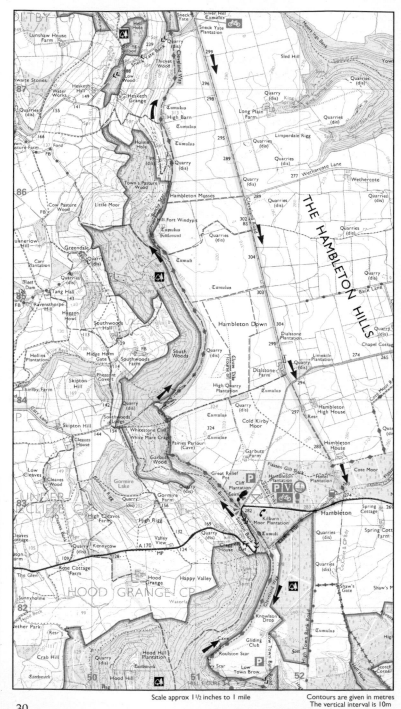

Scale approx 1½ inches to 1 mile

Contours are given in metres
The vertical interval is 10m

A CIRCULAR WALK FROM SUTTON BANK

8½ miles (13.7 km)

This walk covers the section of the Cleveland Way from the White Horse to Sneck Yate. A circular route is achieved by following the old Hambleton Drove Road (now a tarmac road in parts) from a point near Sneck Yate to the Hambleton Inn (originally a drovers' inn) where the Cleveland Way is rejoined to reach the White Horse.

Start from the car park at the top of Sutton Bank, and follow the Cleveland Way northwards to Sneck Yate. At Sneck Yate Bank turn right uphill and at the road junction turn right along the Cleveland road.

Pass Dialstone Farm on your right and at the road junction cross over the road and take a path immediately ahead alongside the fence line passing Hambleton High House on your left. The path leads on to the Hambleton House driveway where you rejoin the Cleveland Way. Continue on the Cleveland Way to reach the Hambleton Inn, the White Horse and your eventual return to Sutton Bank.

The Victorian White Horse at Kilburn, which is best viewed from a distance.

Helmsley

Although a view of the castle 1 is largely lost from within the centre of Helmsley, there are some tempting glimpses of the gaunt ruins from the approach roads into the town. The ruination of Helmsley Castle was achieved deliberately three centuries ago. During the English Civil War the attacking Parliamentarians 'slighted' the castle with cannon fire at the end of a three-month siege in 1644 so that it could never again be used as a fortification.

Helmsley was ruled by a Norman overlord from the time of the Conquest (1066) but it was not until Robert de Roos, the 7th Lord of Helmsley, appeared in 1186 that the earliest foundations of a castle were built.

The castle is built on a natural outcrop of rock, an ideal site. The keen military mind of de Roos executed some spectacular defences with the excavation of two ditches and a massive earth mound between them. This formidable castle held out successfully for three months when it was besieged by the Parliamentary forces in 1644. The Royalists surrendered with dignity only after a relief column was defeated.

Feversham memorial

Dominating the centre of Helmsley's large market place is the Victorian monument 2 which surrounds the statue of William, 2nd Baron Feversham, who died in 1867. This extremely ornate monument was designed by Sir George Gilbert Scott with all the Victorian zeal of the Gothic Revival style. Five years earlier, Scott had completed the even more elaborate Albert Memorial in London.

The natural elements have sadly caused some erosion of the limestone statue, which was created by Mathew Noble, a Yorkshire sculptor, and depicts the baron in the full regalia of his title.

All Saints' Church

The imposing pinnacled tower of the church 3 appears above a screen of churchyard trees. Like many churches it has been extended, remodelled and rebuilt over the centuries according to changes in requirements and architectural fashion. What we see today is largely the work of rebuilding in the 19th century (1866–9) but is none the less fascinating for a number of items of interest which it contains. Norman architecture is revealed in

The Cleveland Way passes by Griff Lodge, above Jinny York Bank. A 'griff' is a deep narrow gully such as that formed by the River Rye flowing below.

the church's fine doorway and the large chancel archway, which has 28 faces carved on its outer ring, all with their tongues rudely stuck out.

The Rev. Charles Gray served at All Saints' for 43 years (1870–1913). He was noted for his zeal in both spiritual and secular matters and was responsible for the fascinating collection of wall paintings and stained-glass windows which tell the story of Christianity from the days of St Columbia to the 19th century. The five windows in the north aisle illustrate aspects of the life of Walter L'Espec, third Lord Helmsley, from 1120 to 1154.

Duncombe Park

For 500 years the owner of the Helmsley estate generally resided in the domestic buildings which were built within the castle grounds. However, in 1713 Thomas Duncombe decided to build a mansion house in the parkland 4 which surrounded the western side of the town. It is quite likely that Vanbrugh, the

The valley of the River Rye with the ruins of Rievaulx Abbey.

leading architect of the time, was called in for advice, but William Wakefield was the architect who was actually given the job of designing the great house. He provided a mansion comprising a large rectangular block and two wings. Attractive lawns, gardens and temples were built, one at each end of a lawned terrace. In the 19th century, the house was altered, suffered two fires and then was finally reconstructed in 1895. The architect largely followed the original plans, so that the house today is not much different from that of 1713.

For a period of 60 years Duncombe Park served as a school for girls, but in 1985 Lord Feversham decided to take up residence in his ancestral home. Plans for extensive renovation were put in hand and the house and parkland are now open to the public. Details of the opening times are available from Helmsley Tourist Information Centre.

Rievaulx Abbey

The ruins of Rievaulx Abbey **5** are indeed among the most beautiful in England and the richly wooded valley of the River Rye provides an equally magnificent setting. Following the Norman Conquest of England in 1066, a large number of religious houses were founded by the Norman overlords who invited groups of monks to come over from France.

In 1131 Walter L'Espec, the Lord of Helmsley, granted some land at Rievaulx to the Cistercian community of Clairvaux in France. The following year a group of 13 white-garbed, shaven-headed monks arrived to set about building what became the largest Cistercian monastery in England. The success of their venture can be judged in no small part by what we see today – impressive as it is in its ruined state, how much more so to those who viewed the monastery some 800 years ago.

As you note the skill of the 12th-century stonemasons you may also wonder at the great wealth required to finance such an undertaking. Apart from endowments bestowed upon the monasteries by the Norman aristocracy, the Cistercians entered the world of commerce through their activities as sheep farmers. The Cistercian rule required the priest-monks to attend services seven times a day and yet be self-sufficient from their own labours on the land. To achieve the impossible, the Cistercians introduced a second class of monks called lay brothers, who worshipped only at the start and finish of their working day. Rievaulx's great wealth was due to the lay brothers, who developed a sheep farming enterprise with over 14,000 sheep on the moors around Rievaulx and Bilsdale. Cloth merchants from Flanders, France and Italy came over each year to purchase wool from English markets including Rievaulx.

The monastery at Rievaulx grew at a phenomenal pace during its early years. In just over 30 years the community grew to 650 men, of which 150 were priest-monks and the remainder lay brothers and abbey servants. During its heyday, Rievaulx was led by St Ailred, the third abbot (1147–67), whose saintly reputation was esteemed throughout Europe.

From about 1300 the fortunes of Rievaulx were on the decline. England was devastated by the Black Death (1348–9 was its most lethal year), the population was cut by one-third and the number of monks slumped dramatically. Rievaulx's inglorious end came in 1538 with the Dissolution of the monasteries under Henry VIII. The king was jealous of their land, wealth and allegiance to Rome and saw an easy means of remedying the low state of his finances. In common with most monastic foundations, Rievaulx was stripped of its treasures inside, its lead roof outside, and was left to the vagaries of nature and some local use of its building stone. In December 1538 the last abbot and his 21 monks found themselves without a home.

Rievaulx Bridge

The original stone bridge was constructed in the 13th century by the lay brothers from Rievaulx Abbey and fragments of it have been discovered in the river bed.

Road bridges along the main routeways became the responsibility of the North Riding Quarter Sessions in the late 17th century and Rievaulx Bridge was one of the 84 bridges maintained by the authority in 1700. In 1754 the great Rye Flood destroyed the bridge, which was replaced by the present humpbacked bridge **6**.

Rievaulx Bridge was on the main route westwards out of Helmsley to Sutton Bank. It was used by William Wordsworth and his sister Dorothy in 1802 when they abandoned their coach and decided to walk all the way from Thirsk to Helmsley. They were *en route* from Grasmere in the Lake District to visit William's future wife, Mary Hutchinson, at Brompton.

Hambleton Down

For over 100 years Hambleton Down **7** was hailed as one of the finest racecourses in England. It is possible that the horse-racing aristocracy of the 18th century found themselves competing here for refreshments with the Highland drovers *en route* to Malton market. Their activities coincided near Sutton Bank and only two drovers' inns (Hambleton and Dialstone) were available at this isolated location. The Hambleton Inn, alongside the Cleveland Way, continues its trade today but Dialstone is now a farm.

Horse-racing started on the Hambleton Down in the late 16th century and by 1612 was well established. The site of the course was alongside the drove road and close to the present Dialstone Farm. In the 18th century both Queen Anne and George I gave gold cups to be competed for annually at Hambleton. Daniel Defoe, on his celebrated 'tour', visited the Hambletons in 1742 and commented on the excellence of the races. Shortly afterwards, in 1755, the main attraction – 'The Hundred Guineas' – was transferred to York and this sent the Hambleton course into speedy decline. The last attempt at a race meeting was held in 1811 with sufficient entrants for just one day's racing.

There are still racing stables in operation and horses are exercised on the short limestone turf of the Hambleton gallops as they have been for 400 years.

White Horse at Kilburn

The presence of a turf-cut figure on the hillside above Kilburn cannot be appreciated from the escarpment edge on the Cleveland Way – it is too massive. Measuring 314 feet (96 metres) long and 228 feet (70 metres) high, the White Horse 8 is a well-known North Yorkshire landmark and best viewed from a distance. It is possible for 20 people to stand on the grass eye of the horse, but visitors are asked not to walk on the surface.

A number of turf-cut figures appear on the chalk downlands of southern England. It is likely that they were the inspiration for Thomas Taylor's suggestion that a horse be cut on the hillside near his native Kilburn. The idea became a reality through the efforts of the local schoolmaster, John Hodgson, who drew a plan and staked an outline on the hill with the help of his pupils. In 1857 it took 30 local volunteers two months to clear the scrub, remove the turf and treat the exposed rock with a coat of lime.

The camber on the hillside makes the White Horse unstable and susceptible to weathering and erosion. Over the past 100 years it has needed restoration from time to time and occasional grooming with white paint and chalk chippings to brighten its appearance. As you stand above this landmark, keep a sharp eye out for another which lies 20 miles (32 km) to the south: the central tower of York Minster.

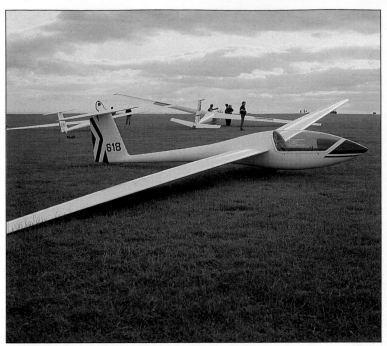

Sutton Bank provides an ideal location for gliding.

Gliding

The Cleveland Way follows a remarkably flat stretch of the Tabular Hills as it skirts round the edge of a natural amphitheatre from Roulston Scar to Whitestone Cliff. It is here that nature has provided a combination of circumstances which make it an ideal site for gliding 9. The prevailing winds and the shape of the land result in the westerly winds being funnelled into strong up-currents as they rise up the sheer face of the bank. The gliders can rise to over 1,000 feet (300 metres) on this local hill lift. Pockets of warm air (thermals) also rise in columns from the semi-circular bowl and pilots can circle for many hours in these rising columns. The westerly winds which pass over the Pennines also form air waves at a high level and gliders can travel for miles along the length of these waves when they reach Sutton Bank. The club altitude record stands at 31,000 feet (9,455 metres).

Soaring gliders fill the sky on some days and provide a spectacle for the visitors to Sutton Bank. The Yorkshire Gliding Club was established here in 1931 and visitors are welcome at the gliding station. Short flights and residential courses can be booked if you wish to experience the world of wind-borne flight.

Hood Hill

The almost conical Hood Hill **10** stands like an extinct volcano separated from the main escarpment of Roulston Scar. It owes its origin to a capping of hard rock which has proved more resistant to weathering than the surrounding underlying beds. The separation of this outlier from the Tabular escarpment was accentuated towards the end of the Ice Age. Meltwater from the moorland snowfields drained southwards, cutting a small valley between the escarpment edge and the glacier-blocked lowland.

The view from Sutton Bank suggests that Hood Hill would make the ideal site for an easily defended castle. There are, in fact, traces of a medieval fortification on the hill, which have supported the record of a Hood Castle in the area during the 12th century. Unfortunately the remains of the castle earthworks are very overgrown and Hood Hill hides its secrets behind a mantle of coniferous trees.

Sutton Bank

The North York Moors has a distinct physical boundary on its western side, set by the escarpment edge of the Hambleton and Cleveland Hills. It is this edge that is followed relentlessly by the Cleveland Way and it provides a line of superb vantage points from which to view the western plains. Any approach from the west involves a steep climb to negotiate this barrier and none more so than the notorious ascent up Sutton Bank **11**. Climbing at a gradient of 1 in 4 in places, even modern cars can overheat in slow-moving traffic by the time they reach the top.

William and Dorothy Wordsworth sat here in 1802 and marvelled at the magnificence of the view, and from the pen of Yorkshire's famous vet, James Herriot, we have a claim for the finest views in England. In the summer sun Gormire Lake glistens like a jewel 500 feet (152 metres) below the edge, and the rocks of Roulston Scar and Whitestone Cliff take on a creamy mantle. Across 20 miles (32 km) of rich farmland to the west your eye touches on the backbone of England, the Pennines, with the conspicuous peaks of Great Whernside and Penhill. Some 35 miles (53 km) to the south, the cooling towers of the Ferrybridge Power Station can be seen on a clear day.

Gormire Lake glistening below Sutton Bank, renowned for its magnificent view

2 Sutton Bank to Osmotherley

via Sneck Yate and Black Hambleton
11½ miles (18.5 km)

This section provides a level walk along the western escarpment edge of the Hambleton Hills overlooking the Vale of York. A good part of the section – from High Paradise to Black Hambleton – follows the route of the Hambleton Drove Road used by the cattle men (drovers) in the 18th and 19th centuries. From Black Hambleton you drop down to the idyllic setting of Oakdale's reservoirs *en route* for Osmotherley.

Leaving Sutton Bank, the Trail continues along the escarpment with a pleasant view down on to Gormire Lake **12**. This relic of the Ice Age is the only natural lake on the North York Moors. The route is straightforward and the walking easy, with commanding views for companionship.

Just beyond the high point above Gormire Lake is Whitestone Cliff (or White Mare Crag) **13**, a place that features in many local legends. Rock climbing occasionally takes place on its 120-foot (36-metre) face. The path then follows a huge arc with South Woods below and the flat grassland of the Hambleton Down **7** to your right.

Ignore any signs to Hambleton Road around the rim, and keep to the top path to reach Boltby Scar. A low grass-covered mound and ditch are all that remain of an Iron Age hill fort **14**. The word Windypits **15** on the map describes the fissures and hollows alongside the path, which are an interesting feature of the local limestone.

Towards the northern end of the scar leave the edge to go through a gate and follow the path bounded by a wall and fence line **A**. This is safer than the edge above Boltby Quarry, one of the many disused limestone quarries **16** in the area. Once through the next gate continue alongside the stone wall in the direction of High Barn.

Past High Barn and its shelterbelt of trees there is a wide grass field. The sheep-grazed limestone turf makes for pleasant walking as you follow the semi-derelict stone wall for a while. The trail leaves the field boundary **B** and descends slightly left and downhill to reach the farm gate and stile in the north wall. As you near the end of this long field, Boltby Reservoir comes into view below a wide sweep of conifer plantations.

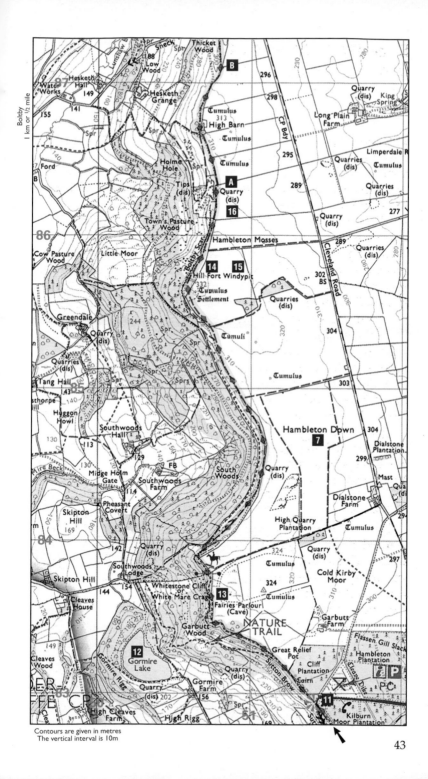

Contours are given in metres
The vertical interval is 10m

43

The Trail leads to Sneck Yate – locally pronounced 'yat' and meaning gate. Cross straight over the Sneck Yate road and follow the obvious path through the small forestry plantation. Emerge from the plantation through a gate on to a green lane, continuing ahead to reach the farm road above Low Paradise Farm. Turn right up the gated road. This is a steep climb through the wooded hillside. Do not take the level track off to the left, halfway up the hill, but continue up the road and then past High Paradise Farm. The farm road leads to a T-junction with the Hambleton Road **C** where you turn left and northwards along this wide green track.

Archaeological finds indicate that the Hambleton Road **17** has been used for thousands of years, back to the Bronze Age and possibly earlier. In more recent times, Scottish drovers brought their cattle along here, hence the name Drove or Drovers' Road.

The Trail takes you along a wide track at the eastern edge of the Boltby Forest. Leave the forest by a gate and proceed on to Little Moor. Immediately through the gate and on the right is the shaft of Steeple Cross **18**. The Drove Road keeps close company with the stone wall.

A long barrow (burial mound) is discernible in the heather over the wall **19**. Although these moors abound in round barrows belonging to the Bronze Age there are very few long barrows of the earlier Neolithic or New Stone Age.

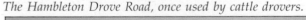
The Hambleton Drove Road, once used by cattle drovers.

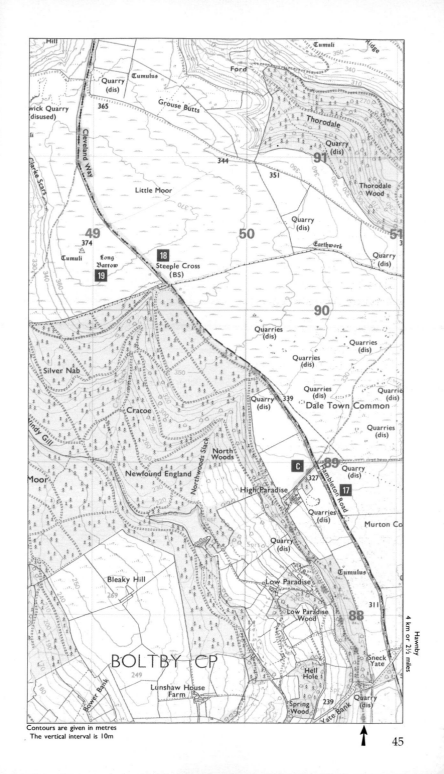

Contours are given in metres
The vertical interval is 10m

45

As you enter a wide enclosed stretch of the route, the pile of stones on the right **D** is all that remains of Limekiln House. This was one of the drovers' inns and was also associated with the limestone industry. At the end of the enclosed section **E** you emerge once again on to the edge of the open moor. At White Gill Head **F** the route takes a left turn and continues in a north-westerly direction round the shoulder of Black Hambleton.

A line of shooting butts **20** appears on the right, composed simply of short sections of stone wall with turf on top. There will, no doubt, be a number of times on this walk when you will see the grouse with their dark, reddish brown plumage and hear their calls of 'ge'back, ge'back'.

The descent from Black Hambleton marks a change in the geology – you now leave the limestone belt behind and move northwards on to sandstone, grits and shales.

On reaching the sharp bend in the unfenced road (Osmotherley to Hawnby), the route branches off left **G** away from the road and through the bracken. Soon you will see the wooded setting of Oak Dale Reservoir and the red pantile roofs of Osmotherley behind. The last stretch downhill crosses a wet flush over stone flags to enter the woodland. Turn right to the footbridge over Jenny Brewster's Beck and follow the track along the edge of Oak Dale's upper reservoir.

At the western end of this reservoir, cross over the stile and continue through the middle of the field along the vehicle access track. This leads down to the left of Oak Dale House (*see map on page 48*). After crossing the bridge over Slape Stones Beck at the corner of the lower reservoir, the track leads uphill. Follow this track to emerge on to the Osmotherley to Hawnby road.

Turn left down the road for a few yards and then sharp right **H** up the farm road signposted Cleveland Way. The official path continues past the farm gateway **I** for just a few yards, then turns left through a sheep sneck in the wall, going downhill to rejoin the farm road – to complete two sides of a triangle!

The Trail bears right on approaching White House Farm. Keep the farm and buildings on the left and proceed across the field, downhill, to reach a stile. Continue downhill near to the right-hand-side field boundary, over the farm track, to reach the footbridge over Cod Beck. The path winds uphill through a delightful woodland edge to emerge into a field. Cross the field in the direction of the church tower and go across the next field to reach a sheep sneck. Follow the well-defined pathway

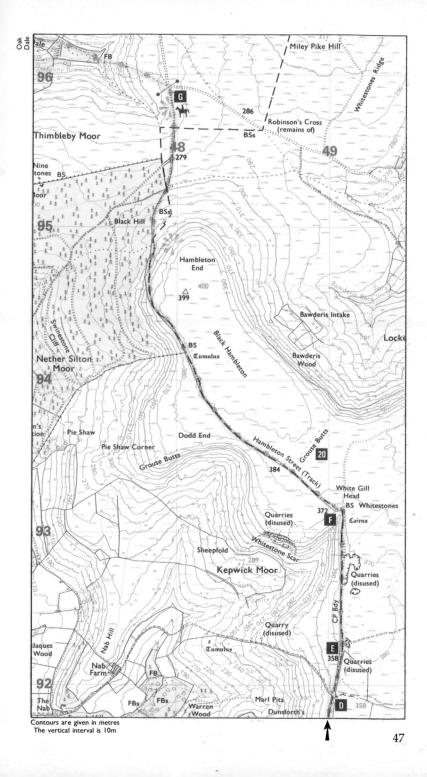

Contours are given in metres
The vertical interval is 10m

47

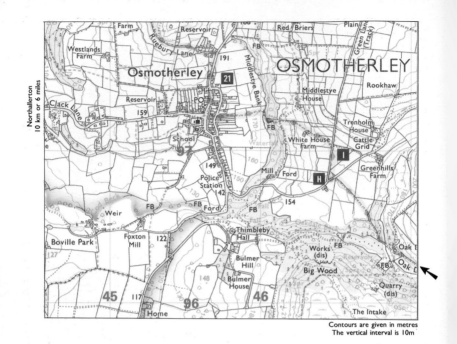

Contours are given in metres
The vertical interval is 10m

alongside the hedge to reach Back Lane. Opposite is a private-looking passage with a flagged path. Follow this through an enclosed passage to the main street of Osmotherley **21**.

A CIRCULAR WALK USING THE DROVE ROAD
7½ miles (12 km)

Start from the village of Osmotherley. There is no car park in the village but roadside parking is adequate. Follow the Cleveland Way from Osmotherley to Scarth Nick (see pages 60–2 for route description). On approaching the road at Scarth Nick turn right and walk south along the road. (If you cut the corner, as shown on the map, you will save a little distance but miss Scarth Nick.)

Cross the footbridge over the beck and follow the broad track uphill. You now continue south along the old route of the Hambleton Drove Road (High Lane) towards Black Hambleton. The track eventually becomes a tarmac road and you continue ahead, past Chequers Farmhouse (an old drovers' inn), to the sharp left-hand bend in the road at point **G** on the map. Turn right here into the bracken and follow the Cleveland Way back into the village of Osmotherley.

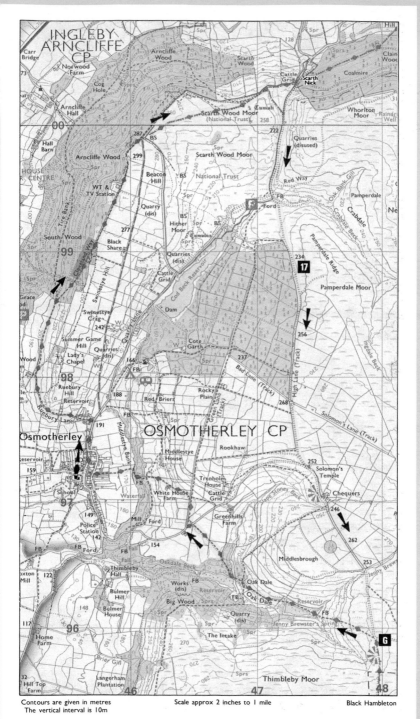

Contours are given in metres
The vertical interval is 10m

Scale approx 2 inches to 1 mile

Black Hambleton

49

Gormire Lake

This is the only natural lake **12** of any significance in the North York Moors National Park. If you stand on the escarpment edge at Sutton Bank, the lake lies 500 feet (152 metres) below. In the midday sun it can sparkle like a diamond, but at other times it takes on a sombre and forbidding mood, giving rise to weird and wicked legends of a bottomless lake where a whole village lies drowned. Set among wooded banks it is a favourite haunt of botanists, and one of its rarities is the yellow-flowering tufted loosestrife. The sheltered stretch of water is a watering ground for several species of waterfowl and a breeding place for wild duck, coot and sometimes the great crested grebe.

The lake is fed by springs emerging in marshy ground along its eastern shore but there is no visible outlet. It drains underground to reappear a few miles further south. The origin of Gormire Lake dates back 10,000 years to the end of the Ice Age when the Vale of York was glacier-filled, several hundred yards thick, from the moors to the Pennines in the west. Meltwater from the moors coursed a channel between the ice and the moor edge. The trench below Sutton Bank was blocked by a late glacial landslide, thus leading to the creation of Gormire Lake.

Whitestone Cliff

Overshadowing Gormire Lake is the 70-foot (21-metre) vertical face of Whitestone Cliff **13** which provides a landmark for motorists approaching from the west via Thirsk. The cliff face is divided into large blocks, roughly cube-shaped, which reveal the strongly-jointed and fissured characteristics of the mainly limestone rock. Where the rock breaks off afresh it has a light creamy tinge but otherwise it weathers to dull grey. Whitestone Cliff has a history of rock falls, the most famous being in March 1755 when the massive falls of rock were so violent that the journals of the day printed reports of a local earthquake. In May of that year John Wesley visited the site and concluded that God had signalled his power to those who foolishly gambled time and money at the adjacent Hambleton racecourse **7**.

The alternative name of White Mare Crag may also owe its origin to the colour of the cliff. After the rock fall of 1755, the newly revealed face was so bright that when seen from a distance its shape appeared like a white horse. Other tales explain the name in more sinister vein – like that of the local knight who was strangely challenged to a midnight race by the

The vertical face of Whitestone Cliff with its mainly limestone rock divided into large blocks.

Abbot of Rievaulx. The abbot exchanged horses and the white mare bolted with its rider over the cliff into Gormire Lake below. As he fell, the knight looked up and saw the wicked abbot change into the likeness of the devil.

The Iron Age

The introduction of implements made of iron came with a wave of immigrants who arrived in North Yorkshire around 650 BC and whose way of life continued until the Roman invasion of this area in AD 70. We know from pollen analyses that the climate took an abrupt turn for the worse around 500 BC and settlements on the cold damp moors were abandoned for the kinder confines of the dales.

The Iron Age people were grouped in sufficiently well-organised communities to carry out the almost inevitable consequence of tribal division: warfare. There are two earthworks – on Roulston Scar and Boltby Scar – discovered along the Cleveland Way which have been described as promontory hill forts dating from the Iron Age. Roulston fort, discovered in 1969, has a few remains but Boltby fort **14** is now represented only by a grass-covered mound and ditch. Sadly, two-thirds of the Boltby fort were destroyed by ploughing in 1961.

51

Boltby Scar provides a natural defensive site with the scarp edge on two sides of a triangle. The third side was protected by a ditch and raised rampart.

Windypits

Windypits is the local name given to the wide cracks (fissures) which appear in the Corallian limestone and usually lead to some small cavern or pit. The name is derived from the fact that in warm weather cold air currents rise up the fissures and often escape with enough velocity to shake the surrounding vegetation. In cold weather, the relatively warmer air escapes from the holes as vapour.

The slight acidity of rainwater is sufficient to dissolve limestone slowly along its joints and bedding planes. Although there are no caves, caverns or potholes to compare in size with those in the Yorkshire Dales, the Corallian limestone has developed a number of sizeable fissures. Although we can easily appreciate that ground-level caves would have provided prehistoric people with convenient shelter, it is surprising to find that they also inhabited the windypits. The Beaker people of the New Stone Age (around 2000 BC) descended these fissures to a depth of 80 feet (24 metres) to make temporary homes, presumably in winter, and also to bury their dead. These facts came to light, through the efforts of local archaeologists, only in the 1950s.

Limestone

The influence of limestone is apparent along the Cleveland Way from the start in Helmsley's market place to the northern edge of Black Hambleton. This well-drained rock gives rise to the short springy turf at your feet and the thin but fertile brown soil of the farmland. The limestone beds have provided a source of stone for local buildings, road making and the production of agricultural lime.

The Hambleton Hills are composed essentially of limestones interbedded with some fine-grained sandstones. Around Helmsley the houses often exhibit a honey-coloured stone where the impure limestone contains a proportion of sand and iron. In the summer they give a warm hue to the landscape.

The limestone gives rise to a thin layer of easily-worked soil. The soil nutrients, including calcium, are soon leached, however, and the land must be limed, so limestone was quarried, crushed and burnt to produce lime for the fields.

Small disused quarries are numerous and many farms had their own quarry and lime-burning kiln. The demand for agricultural lime also gave rise to trade with other parts of the Moors. Today, the quarrying of limestone is concentrated in a few large quarries lying on the limestone belt between Helmsley and Scarborough.

Hambleton Drove Road

This is a 15-mile (24-km) routeway over the Hambleton Hills which is followed in part by the Cleveland Way between Sutton Bank and Osmotherley. The road **17** takes its name from the Scottish cattlemen (drovers) who were hired to drive cattle all the way from Scotland and across the English countryside to sell at various market towns as far south as London. The Hambleton Drove Road was just one of many routes which were followed by these tough, weather-beaten traders.

Although this ridgeway route is best remembered as a great cattle road, it has been used as far back as prehistoric times. Flints, axes and pottery from the Stone Age have been found along the route, and on Kepwick Moor there is a rare long barrow (burial mound) of the period **19**.

Droving owed its existence to the market forces to supply and demand. The demand for beef in the growing towns of the 18th century could not be met by the English farmers. The Industrial Revolution of the late 18th and early 19th-century aggravated the demand for fresh meat from the rapidly expanding industrial towns. This meant busy times for the sheep and cattle farmers of Scotland and Wales and many miles of walking for the drovers (three or four times round the Cleveland Way for a round-trip equivalent!). The inventiveness of the Industrial Revolution did, however, sound the death knell of droving. Steam power replaced leg power and the 19th-century railway network soon made it possible to slaughter beasts locally and send the carcasses to market from all over the land. Droving was in decline from the 1850s, and by 1900 it had ceased entirely.

You will not meet cattle 'on the hoof' along the Hambleton Drove Road today, but at Sutton Bank you cross the point where in July 1802 William and Dorothy Wordsworth rested from their toil up the hill. As luck would have it some drovers were there and Dorothy records in her *Journal* that 'the sun shone hot, the little Scottish cattle panted and tossed fretfully about'. From Sutton Bank those drovers would most likely have continued to the market at either Malton or York.

Kepwick Quarry showing the disused incline tramway.

54

The cross known as Fat Betty stands on the moors above Rosedale Head.

Moorland crosses and other standing stones

These stones are an unmistakable feature of the moorland scene. There are over 30 named moorland crosses on the North York Moors and it is likely that no other part of Britain can boast of such a concentration. As a symbol of Christ's death, the cross has been used on the North York Moors since the 7th-century flowering of Christianity in the region. The oldest Christian monument in northern England is said to be Lilla Cross, which stands atop an earlier Bronze Age burial mound on Fylingdales Moor. This isolated site was chosen to commemorate the death in 626 of Lilla, who is reputed to have saved King Edwin of Northumbria from an assassin's dagger and been mortally wounded as a result of his own brave action.

The particular importance of stone moorland crosses on the North York Moors was recognised in 1974 when the National Park Committee chose Ralph Cross as its emblem. Standing almost in the geographical centre of the Moors, Ralph Cross is an imposing monument seen by everyone as they motor from Hutton-le-Hole to Castleton.

Many of the crosses are without the cross-piece and consist of nothing more than a base, stump or simple pillar. Some crosses will undoubtedly have been erected as waymarkers, dating as far back as the medieval period, to guide the weary traveller across the desolate moors. Placed on strategic points, these waymarkers link together to provide an indication of ancient routeways. There are a number of waymarkers of a later date, some of which will be seen alongside the Cleveland Way. Mostly of 18th-century origin, these waymarkers are inscribed with the names of destinations and some have a roughly carved hand indicating the direction, hence the name 'handstones'.

A large number of moorland stones were erected as boundary markers relating to parish or land ownership boundaries. In addition to individual sites, regular lines of these stone boundary markers can be seen on the moors, some bearing the initials of villages or of the lords of the manor who erected them.

In his book on standing stones on the North York Moors, Stanhope White describes just a selection of the 1,500 sites he visited while recording these historic characters.

New Stone Age

The study of prehistory attempts to determine, in broad measures, how the main features of life progressed and changed over thousands of years. Changes in implements, tools, pottery, burial mounds and methods of agriculture are among the measures we use to determine the changes in culture from one period to another.

The culture represented by the New Stone Age (Neolithic) lasted nearly 2,500 years. It marked a change from the hunter-gatherer economy to farming, with a more settled and organised method of land use and animal husbandry. The main aspects of this culture spread across our area over a period from 4300 BC to 2000 BC.

The only evidence you will actually see of these ancestors as you walk the Cleveland Way will be the long low bump in the heather on Kepwick Moor **19**. The long barrow (burial mound) was the New Stone Age method of burial. Several corpses were burnt in a stone-lined trench and then covered with earth and rubble. There are only a handful of Neolithic sites in the area but their long barrows are the oldest man-made structures on the North York Moors. The beautifully decorated Beaker pottery, usually associated with the Bronze Age in Europe, was found in the Neolithic burial chambers of the Windypits **15**, dated at around 2000 BC.

Moorland

The distinctive character of the North York Moors lies in its moorland. This central heartland provides the largest extent of heather moorland in England and covers some 40 per cent of the North York Moors National Park. For much of the year its dark brown rolling landscape is bleak and wild, broken only by the softer intervening dales. Late summertime magic transforms the moor into a sea of purple haze as the heather bursts into bloom. It has been estimated that there are 3,000 million flowers in every square mile of heather (nearly two million per hectare). The Cleveland Way touches the wildness and freedom of these moors along the western flank of the Cleveland Hills from Osmotherley to Kildale. There are glimpses *en route* into the green-fingered dales of Bilsdale, Bransdale, Farndale and Esk Dale.

Animal and bird life will not escape your notice – in the form of sheep and grouse. They are both an essential part of the moorland scene. The 'Swaledale' is a hardy breed of sheep easily distinguished by its black face, speckled nose and speckled legs. The ewes have single-curved horns while the tups (rams) can have double- or triple-curved horns. Despite the lack of boundary fences, the flocks keep to their own strays (territories); they are what the farmer calls 'heafed to the moor'. Ear, horn and paint marks are all used to distinguish the sheep belonging to a particular farm.

The lines of shooting butts **20** are a reminder of the grouse-shooting season between 12 August and 10 December. During a shoot you may see a line of beaters raising the birds in the direction of the shooters; you should take care to keep strictly to the path while the shooting is in progress.

The management of the moor for the last 100 years or so has amounted to little more than the deliberate burning of the heather. The old woody heather is burnt off in patches to encourage young green shoots to appear, which provide a more nutritious feed for both sheep and grouse.

Osmotherley

Osmotherley **21** holds a slightly elevated position at the edge of the Moors, with the Cleveland Hills to the north and the Hambleton Hills to the south. It is likely that the name of the village derived from 'Asmundrelac' as recorded in the Domesday Book (1086). Asmund is an Old Norse personal name and this was 'Asmund's clearing'. Later influences (Anglian) often resulted in place-name changes from 'As' to 'Os'. This is a more rational explanation than the legend of the drowning Prince Oswy (see page 91).

The settlement has developed primarily as an agricultural market village but during the 18th and 19th centuries it was also a thriving industrial centre. It provided accommodation for workers in the local alum quarries and jet mines, and was a centre for the weaving and bleaching industry based on the mills which used the water power of Cod Beck. The present youth hostel at Cote Ghyll was a busy linen mill which finally closed in 1915. Many of the small attractive cottages in Osmotherley were built to house the growing number of workers in the period 1800–30 when the population doubled from 500 to over 1,000.

There are two main streets running at right angles, with a small village green at the T-junction. Here are Osmotherley's trademarks which appear on the picture postcards – the market cross and a stone table standing on squat stone pillars.

The table would no doubt be useful on market days and also as a resting place for coffins *en route* to the church. John Wesley stood on the table to preach during one of his many visits.

Anyone with an interest in churches will appreciate the parish church. Although largely the result of Victorian zeal for remodelling, it retains a fine 15th-century porch containing some 12th-century stones with Scandinavian chain-plait carving.

For more than 100 years Osmotherley has been a haven for holidaymakers and day-trippers. It is also now home for many commuters working in the county town of Northallerton and the industrial complex of Teesside.

The pagan custom of celebrating midsummer may account for the origin of the Osmotherley Summer Games, one of the highlights of the village year. They are now held in the village, but at one time the venue was Summer Game Hill (still marked on the map) near the Lady Chapel.

3 Osmotherley to Clay Bank

via Scarth Nick and Carlton Bank
11 miles (18 km)

This is the most strenuous section of the Trail, where the Cleveland Hills are broken into a succession of moors between Huthwaite Green and Clay Bank. For the most part, when the skies are clear, the route and the views will be among the most memorable. Take care in descending the steeper slopes, and beware the onset of cold north-easterlies along the moor tops.

Walk uphill through the village along the road signposted to Swainby. At the top of the hill **A** turn left along Ruebury Lane. The lane eventually becomes a farm track, climbing for a short distance then circling Ruebury Hill on a level course. Do not take the path branching off to the right and uphill unless you wish to make a short detour to visit the Lady Chapel **22**.

Ruebury Hill provides an extensive panorama of the Vale of York with the sight and frenzied sounds of the A19 in the foreground below. A feeling of 'better here than there' is understandable from this point!

There is a 1-mile (1.6-km) detour via Chapel Wood Farm **B** if you wish to visit Mount Grace Priory **23**, which has the most extensive remains of any Carthusian monastery in Britain. The footpath to Mount Grace leads down through the farmyard; you must retrace your steps to rejoin the Cleveland Way.

The Trail continues past Chapel Wood Farm, through the gate and straight ahead along the farm track at the bottom edge of the field.

Immediately through the gate into South Wood turn right **C** along the track leading uphill through the forestry plantation. The clay subsoil of this hillside is clearly revealed in a couple of ditches. The track here is a long haul to the top, but you will achieve a commanding view when the route emerges on to a patch of heather, bilberry and scrub woodland.

The path continues along the level top through the scrub woodland. The escarpment edge of Beacon Hill is bedecked with all the technological ironmongery of a British Telecom television booster station. This is a somewhat incongruous conglomeration of hardware for a national park, but necessary for modern communications. The enclosed section of path between the stone wall and perimeter fence leads you past the television station. A short distance along is an Ordnance Survey

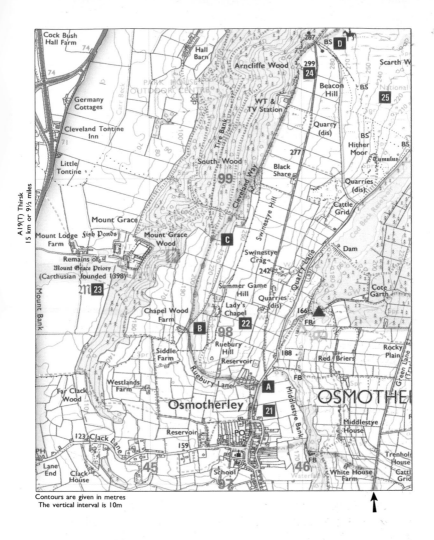

Contours are given in metres
The vertical interval is 10m

triangulation pillar, over the wall, marking the summit of Beacon Hill at 981 feet (299 metres). This point is the start of the famous Lyke Wake Walk **24** which leads across 40 miles (64 km) of moorland to the coast at Ravenscar.

The nab ends, or promontories, of the Cleveland Hills come into view. The small outlier ahead is Whorl Hill which lies near the village of Swainby. As the path descends you leave the forest area by a gate and then go through another gate on to Scarth Wood Moor which is owned by the National Trust **25**. Take the path **D** which leads across the heather moor, bisecting the angle of the immediate boundary walls.

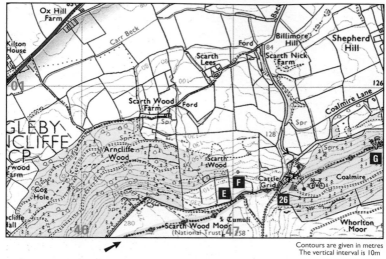

Contours are given in metres
The vertical interval is 10m

As you descend Scarth Wood Moor, the village of Swainby and its church steeple come into view to the north. The path meets the corner of a stone wall boundary **E**. This fine example of the craft of stone walling was completed in 1988 by a Community Programme team. You now leave the track where it swings round to the right **F** and descend alongside the stone wall to reach Scarth Nick via the steps cut in the hillside. Scarth Nick is a glacial overflow channel **26** and also formed part of the Drove Road where it led down off the moor and cut across the Cleveland Plain to Yarm.

On reaching the road turn left, cross the cattle grid and then immediately turn right through a gate into the wood. The path soon joins a forestry track where you continue straight ahead along level ground.

At a break in the forest **G** on the left-hand side there is a delightful view down into the village of Swainby, and at this point you leave the forest track and descend down a wide break on the left. This is a fairly steep slope with an often muddy section at the base. Immediately before the farm gate, turn sharp right down a path which leads you along the pleasant route through a woodland edge.

Where the hardcore path ends **H**, take the stile on your left into the field. Take a bearing across the field more or less at a right angle to the stile. This leads to a gate and over a footbridge which crosses Piper Beck. On reaching the road turn left, where the road then crosses Scugdale Beck and passes Hollin Hill Farm

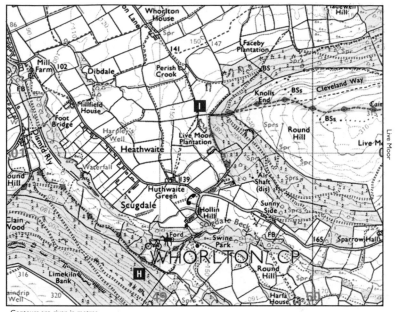

Contours are given in metres
The vertical interval is 10m

to a T-junction. Cross the road here to the right of the telephone box and go through the gate along the enclosed path leading uphill towards Live Moor Plantation.

The hardcore path leads alongside the plantation. Turn right **I**, cross the stile and continue up a steep climb through the trees. There is no respite at the top edge of the plantation as the trail continues uphill, striking the edge of Round Hill. Finally the trail finds a contour at the side of Live Moor along which you can enjoy level walking and open views to the north.

From Live Moor the Trail ahead leading to Carlton Moor is clearly visible. An easy descent from Live Moor is made before the trail leads gently upwards, skirting round Gold Hill and along the edge of Faceby Bank. There are panoramic views of the Cleveland Plain as you walk along the escarpment edge.

An unexpected sight greets you at Carlton Moor. Stripped bare of vegetation, the glider station runway presents a stretch of desert landscape enveloped by heather moorland. Take care here **J** to keep to the edge of the runway nearest to the escarpment. The Trail then takes a left fork to reach the cliff edge **K** and the Ordnance Survey triangulation pillar at 1,338 feet (408 metres), the highest point on Carlton Moor. Below the moor top is the jet miners' track, which roughly follows the 900-foot

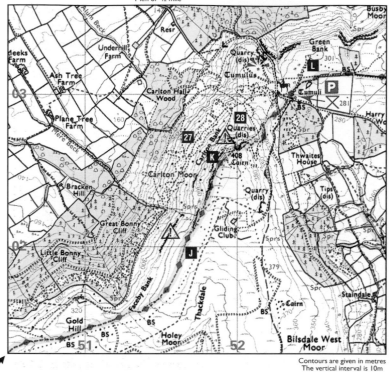

Contours are given in metres
The vertical interval is 10m

(275-metre) contour. The miners excavated along the Cleveland hillsides in their search for small pockets of jet **27** which once gave fame to Whitby where the gemstone was made into jewellery.

The Trail leaves the trig point and descends Carlton Bank to reach the road. The large waste heaps of burnt shale (pink in colour) **28** are a reminder that the alum industry lasted for over 250 years on the North York Moors.

On reaching the road, cross and climb over a stile. The Trail continues along a level path, passing a small copse of trees on the right, to the corner of the fence line **L**. (There is access to the Lord's Stone car park, café and toilets from the Trail, near the copse). Keep the fence line on your right and at the next field corner cross the stile, to follow the path leading uphill towards Cringle Moor.

The Cleveland Way follows a steady climb up to the nab (Cringle End) of Cringle Moor. At the top there is a rewarding view, a welcome stone seat and a boundary stone. The view indicator will direct you to a number of distant landmarks.

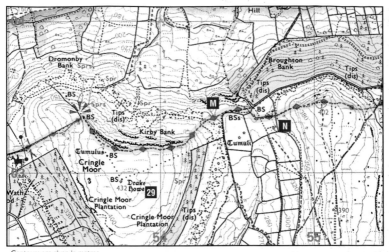

Contours are given in metres
The vertical interval is 10m

Nearer to hand is Captain Cook's Monument on Easby Moor
but another 15 miles (24 km) of walking lies ahead before you
reach the monument. The stone seat on Cringle End was erected
in memory of Alec Falconer who died in 1968. He was one of
the founder members of the Middlesbrough Rambling Club
who promoted the idea of a long-distance holiday walk along
the hills and coast of the North York Moors. Sadly, he died only
one year before the opening of the Cleveland Way.

Drake Howe, a Bronze Age burial mound **29** lies at the top
of Cringle Moor. Although the Trail keeps to the escarpment
edge above Kirby Bank you can note that Drake Howe is the
second highest point at 1,427 feet (432 metres) alongside the
Cleveland Way. The highest is yet to come – on Urra Moor.

All along the escarpment edge of Cringle Moor there are
impressive views over the Cleveland Plain. The paved and
stone-pitched path here replaces an earlier, eroded pathway.

The Trail winds steeply down from Cringle Moor on a stone-
pitched path. You cross the wet flush and the path continues
with a stone wall on the right **M**. At the end of the stone wall,
turn right and cross the stile to follow a wall on the left for 60
yards (55 metres). Turn left with the wall on the left, leading
uphill. Go through the field gate and continue uphill with a
fairly steep climb up on to Cold Moor. The old jet mine entrance
N on the side of the dale has its tell-tale heap of spoil waste
outside. The 'cave' provides a welcome shelter in bad weather.

65

The Wainstones, one of the few local rock climbing areas.

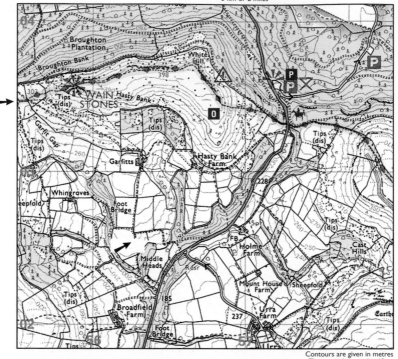

Contours are given in metres
The vertical interval is 10m

Cross the top of Cold Moor and descend through a gate to follow the wall on your right down to Garfit Gap. Ahead now is the climb up Hasty Bank to reach the rock pinnacles of the Wainstones. Various paths find a narrow route between the jumble of boulders and bare rock outcrops. This is one of the few locations on the North York Moors which offers some sport to rock climbers.

Beyond the Wainstones it is plain sailing along the plateau of Hasty Bank. This level stretch is highlighted by the superb views and dramatic cliffs which drop down to the forestry plantation below. Clay Bank car park will be a welcome sight if this is where you intend to break the route and head for overnight accommodation in Great Broughton or Bilsdale.

Where the arc of the cliffs comes to an end **O** the route takes a steep rocky path downhill. Cross over the step-stile and turn immediately right to walk downhill alongside the wall to reach the B1257 Stokesley to Helmsley road. Turn left here if you wish to reach Clay Bank car park **P**.

Lady Chapel

The Chapel of Our Lady of Mount Grace **22** was founded in 1515, reputedly by Catherine of Aragon, the first of Henry VIII's six wives. It is sometimes referred to as Lady Catherine's Chapel, and the Queen Catherine Hotel in Osmotherley echoes this connection. At the Dissolution of the monasteries the Lady Chapel escaped destruction and was given to the last prior of Mount Grace, which was closed in 1539. Over the next 100 years it fell into disrepair but was eventually restored in the 19th century and is now a popular place of pilgrimage.

Mount Grace Priory

Most monastic houses in England were established during the 12th century, but it was not until the late 14th century that Mount Grace Priory **23** was founded (1398). The priory belonged to the Carthusian Order. The monks made a deliberate attempt to reintroduce the solitary way of life as practised by the early religious hermits. Nine Carthusian houses were established in England, and Mount Grace provides the best and most extensive ruins of them all. While it is not a place of great architectural magnificence, like Rievaulx, it does possess an all-pervading sense of the peaceful solitude enjoyed by these 'silent' monks.

The Carthusian monks, under a vow of silence, were housed in small individual cells where they lived, ate and prayed. One of the 20 ruined cells at Mount Grace Priory has been reconstructed. There is a square hole in the wall through which the hermit-like monk was served his meal each day. The hole was deliberately angled so the monk could not see who brought his food. Contact with others was virtually confined to the occasional communal meal and joint services in the church.

The monks lived at Mount Grace for 140 years until the priory was forced to close in 1539 under Henry VIII's Dissolution of the monasteries.

Lyke Wake Walk

For many years the best known of the named walks on the North York Moors was the Lyke Wake Walk **24**. The idea of a west–east walk along the watershed of the Moors was devised by Bill Cowley in 1955. The challenge of completing a 40-mile (64-km) crossing from Osmotherley to Ravenscar within a 24-hour period fired the imagination of many people of all ages and from all over Britain. Sadly, its popularity with thousands of walkers each year, including many sponsored charity walks, resulted in the serious erosion of some parts of the high moors. The National Park Authority set up a working party which requested a voluntary reduction in the number of walkers. In some sections it will take many years for the moorland vegetation to be re-established, particularly where the peat itself has subsequently been eroded by weathering.

Long-distance walking increased greatly in popularity during the 1980s, and there are now plenty of alternative walks where people can meet the challenge either for charity or personal endeavour.

The National Trust

The National Trust is a charitable organisation which is dependent on the public for its membership and support. It was founded to protect the nation's heritage – historic houses, beautiful gardens, unspoilt countryside and coastline, and even entire villages.

The Trust has landowning interests on the Moors and the Cleveland Way passes through a number of them: Scarth Wood Moor **25**, Roseberry Topping **34** and Ravenscar **51**, as well as Port Mulgrave, Saltwick Nab (Whitby), Rocket Post Field (Robin Hood's Bay) and Knipe Point. It also has two properties in the area, Mount Grace Priory and Rievaulx Terrace and Temples, which are close to the route of the walk.

Ice Age

Over the last two million years, icesheets have advanced and retreated at least four times. This lengthy period of alternating warm and ice-cold climatic conditions is known as the Great Ice Age. The refrigeration of the Moors during the last (Devensian) glaciation did not end until about 10,000 years ago, thus making way for recolonisation by plants and animals and for prehistoric people to appear on the scene. The last Ice Age stamped its character firmly around the Moors and some of the effects are readily observed along the Cleveland Way.

The advancing icesheets crunched their way slowly southwards along the eastern and western flanks, with the central belt of the Moors blanketed in permanent snow. When the thaw finally came, meltwater from the moorland snowfield formed lakes in valleys, spilling southwards and outwards where it could. Meltwater action was responsible for the Scarth Nick spillway (north of Osmotherley) **26**, Gormire Lake **12** and for accentuating the isolation of Hood Hill **10**. Deposition of debris from the melting ice plastered the coastal belt with reddish-brown boulder clay – so called because of the large rocks it contains. The instability and easy erosion of this boulder clay demands your attention from time to time on the coastal section of the Cleveland Way.

Jet

Jet gave the town of Whitby remarkable fame, both national and international. Nevertheless, jet jewellery has a much longer history than the 19th-century period of concentrated activity. Jet is the oldest extractive industry on the North York Moors and beads have been discovered in Bronze Age burial mounds dating from 2,500 to 3,500 years ago. It was also highly prized by the Romans and Anglo-Saxons. Jet is a fossilised wood with a very dark, black-brown colour, relatively light in weight, tough but sometimes brittle and capable of an extremely high polish. It was formed about 130 million years ago when pieces of coniferous driftwood were buried by mud in the Jurassic seas. The result is that the jet occurs at random, albeit within a fairly well-defined bed of rocks, and in all shapes and sizes. Although it is usually referred to as 'Whitby jet', pockets of jet have been found elsewhere on the North York Moors where the Jet Rock Series outcrop along the coast, the Cleveland Hills and some inland dales. Some 60 locations were worked for jet in the 19th century.

The modern story of jet production in Whitby began in 1800 when a couple of local men began a partnership in the production of beads and crosses. A retired naval captain introduced them to the art of turning on a lathe, as used with amber. The similarities gave rise to jet's reputation as the 'Black Amber' of Whitby. From then on the jet industry developed gradually, and in 1850 there were 50 jet workshops in Whitby. Jet might never have come particularly to our notice and certainly never achieved the prominence it did, had it not been for Queen Victoria. When her husband Albert, the Prince Consort, died in 1861, the Queen wore masses of jet jewellery and decreed that it should be worn as Court mourning. Jet was already recognised as an emblem of mourning, but with royal patronage the trade received great publicity and a boom period ensued. Within the next 12 years the number of workshops quadrupled to 200 and gave employment to over 1,400 men and

Meltwater during the Ice Ages was responsible for the isolation of Hood Hill.

boys. In addition, 200 miners were engaged in the tedious search for the semi-precious stone. However, fashions change and the popularity of jet was destined to fall. By the 1880s the days of its glory were over and jet was on the decline.

However, the interest in jet has never entirely disappeared. It is still carved in Whitby from rough jet found on the beaches. The Cleveland Way will take you past the miners' spoil heaps, the Whitby craft shops, and to sea level where you can scour the beach for a piece of genuine Whitby jet. It can be distinguished from a piece of sea-washed coal by rubbing it along a light-coloured stone: jet will leave a brown streak whereas coal will leave a black streak.

Alum

There are 25 sites of alum quarries on the North York Moors which were variously active over a period of nearly 300 years from 1600 to 1871. It was the most extensive extractive industry in the history of the area. Nature has not yet been able to disguise the evidence of the massive shale heaps which you will see, for example, at Carlton Bank, Boulby and Sandsend.

The production of alum crystals was an ancient chemical process and a fairly secret one too. The value of alum lay mainly in its property as a mordant or fixative of dyes in cloth. There was a virtual monopoly in the production of alum by Italy during much of the 16th century. However, towards the end of that century a member of the Chaloner family in Britain mastered the process. In 1600 shales containing the mineral alum were first quarried in the Cleveland Hills near Guisborough. Other sites followed and outcrops of the alum shale were exploited along the coast from Saltburn to Ravenscar and along the Cleveland escarpment from Osmotherley to Guisborough.

Apart from its long history, the process required anything from 50 to 100 tons of shale to make just one ton of alum crystals. Millions of tons of shale were extracted, leaving scars on the Cleveland hillsides and dramatically altering parts of the coast.

Those were the days of pick and shovel labour, with packhorses and sailing ships for transport. The shale extracted by the hard-driven, poorly-paid quarrymen was subjected to a long, involved, tedious process ending in a somewhat uncertain chemical result. The shale was piled up into large mounds to burn slowly for up to a year. It was then soaked (leached) in water and the solution boiled, crystallised and purified. The process required brushwood for the burning, water for the leaching, coal for the boiling, seaweed and human urine for the chemistry.

Modern machinery could tear the landscape apart in a fraction of the time taken by the quarrymen. Thankfully, that is not an aspect that we have had to witness in this national park. In the first place a cheaper method of alum production was devised in 1855, treating colliery waste, and, secondly, synthetic dyes which did not need the alum fixative were developed a year later. The long history of alum came to a halt with the closure of the Kettleness and Boulby works in 1871.

Bronze Age

It seems strange to look at an expanse of wild inhospitable moorland and suggest that it once supported a widespread and thriving agricultural community. Yet 4,000 years ago there began a period when these moors were home to our Bronze Age ancestors (2000 BC to 500 BC). The round barrow is the particular hallmark of that period and these burial mounds can be found across the high moors. The Ordnance Survey maps are studded with references to 'howes' and 'tumuli' (alternative names for burial mounds). There are over 3,000 of them on the North York Moors and many have individual names, such as Burton Howe and Drake Howe **29** which lie beside the route off the Cleveland Way. The word 'howe' is derived from an Old Norse word for a grave or mound. The Bronze Age barrows range in size from slight bumps in the heather to mounds measuring 30 yards (27 metres) in diameter and 3 yards (3 metres) high.

Two reasons are given for the eventual abandonment of the plateaux. In the first place, the thin upland soils could not support the impoverishment of their nutrients caused by continuous agriculture. It was a classic case of agricultural robbery. Bronze Age farming had transformed the original tree-covered hills into an infertile heathland. In the second place, pollen analysis indicates a worsening of the climate around 500 BC, hastening an inevitable move to the more sheltered conditions of the dales.

4 Clay Bank to Kildale

via Bloworth Crossing
9¼ miles (15 km)

A fairly level but circuitous route takes you over Round Hill, the highest point on the North York Moors, to the track-bed of a disused railway. The route to Kildale is studded with signs of the past – waymarkers, boundary stones and burial mounds. Many of the burial mounds were excavated in the 19th century; the grave goods were taken but no records were kept.

If you start from Clay Bank car park, walk along the road (B1257) southwards for 300 yards (270 metres) until you reach the hand gate on the left-hand side of the road. Follow the path uphill alongside the wall on your left. The route rises steeply as you test your leg power on the way to the top. When you stop to take a breath, turn round to enjoy the view westwards across Cold Moor, Cringle Moor, Carlton Moor and Live Moor. The spring waters running south feed the infant Bilsdale Beck and with your back to industrial Teesside you have a fine view of the rolling moorland landscape.

The wide stretch of path is crossed at right angles **A** by a line of boundary stones. The gentle rise over Round Hill **B** on Urra Moor could almost go unrecognised as the highest point on the North York Moors. The Ordnance Survey triangulation pillar is 1,489 feet (454 metres) above sea level and lies in the heather, to the left of the path, on top of a Bronze Age burial mound.

To the right of the path (almost opposite the pillar) is the Hand Stone, a guidepost erected in the early 18th century with two crudely carved hands indicating the direction to 'Stoxla' (Stokesley) and 'Kirby' (Kirbymoorside). A short distance along the route on your left is the Face Stone. This ancient boundary marker has a carving of a face on its eastern side.

The Trail continues ahead along the fire-break as it descends gradually to Cockayne Head. Do not take the first track to the right **C** nor the second track to the left **D**. These tracks act as fire-breaks to provide some protection against the spread of uncontrolled moorland fires. In 1976 over 60 fires were recorded in various locations on the North York Moors. Carelessness with a discarded match or cigarette end is the unforgivable cause of such fires in many cases.

The track takes a sharp left turn **E** but the Cleveland Way continues ahead over the headwaters of High Bloworth Beck to meet the track-bed **F** of the old Rosedale Ironstone Railway **30**.

Lawns
Hill
181

West Wood
Farm

Ford
170

High
Farm

Foot
Bridge

84

158

P

P

X

Barnfield
Wood

Midnight
Farm

Plane
Hill

New Sheepfold
Farm

Greenhow
Botton

Foot
Bridge

300

Tips
(dis)

Greenhow
Plantation

Clogger's
Hall

Old Sheepfold
Farm

03

289

Carr Ridge

389

Working (dis)

Jackson Bank

Shepherd
Close

Tips
(dis)

A

BSs

377

Cleveland Way

Cast
Hills

House
rm

Sheepfold

Cowkill
Well

Grouse
Butts

Maiden Spring

Botton
Head

rra
arm

02

Earthwork

Urra Moor

B

Round
Hill

454

Cairns

Urra

Maltkiln House

Tips
(dis)

390

375

Medd
Crag

01

Broad Ings

North Gill
Head

Tips
(dis)

Earthwork

Broad Ings Beck

Collar Ridge

North Gill

400

East Bank
Plantation

Grouse Butts

Fords

Earthwork

Sheepfold

East Bank
House

58

340

59

Tr

Turn right along the track-bed in a south-easterly direction until you come to the crossroads at Bloworth Crossing **G** where you turn sharp left back along the moorland road.

For nearly 70 years (1861–1929) Bloworth Crossing had manned gates to ensure the safety of travellers on the Rudland Rigg road which comes over the moor from Fadmoor to the south-east. Today it is a crossroads for walkers. Those on the Lyke Wake and Coast-to-Coast Walks continue east along the dismantled railway track.

The Cleveland Way continues along the ancient roadway for a further 2½ miles (4 km) before branching off on a right fork at Tidy Brown Hill.

The ancient waymarker **H** known as Jenny Bradley is indecipherable. Many moorland crosses have personal names but no one knows who Jenny was. The second and taller stone here has carvings on three sides: 'F1838' and 'T.A. 1768' indicating landowner's initials and dates of boundary agreements; and 'Sir W. Fowels' who was the 8th baronet of the Ingleby Estate and died in 1845.

If you make a short diversion along the track off to the left **I** you can visit 'Siberia' – at least that was the nickname the railwaymen gave to the tiny group of cottages which existed at Incline Top. The ironstone waggons were let down the incline (1 in 5 to 1 in 11) by gravity, with the empty waggons hauled up by the full ones going down. All traces have disappeared now except the incline and the ruined Drum House.

Just beyond a line of grouse butts is Burton Howe **J**, a notable Bronze Age howe (burial site). There is a group of four burial mounds of which the most southerly, Burton Howe, is some 50 feet (15 metres) in diameter and about 8 feet (2.5 metres) high.

From the viewpoint **K** there is a fine panorama of the Cleveland Plain and also west to Clay Bank car park and the rock scar cliffs of Hasty Bank. The car park is only 2 miles (3.2 km) away as the crow flies, but you have taken a circuitous route of 5½ miles (8.8 km) to reach this point.

The Trail continues along level ground and there is another 18th-century handstone in the heather on the right of the road. The moorland road continues on to Ingleby Greenhow but at Tidy Brown Hill you fork right **L** – there is a metal gate across the path to discourage motor vehicles. The description 'tidy' is said to be a corruption of 'tiddy', meaning small. The path descends gently from Tidy Brown Hill then up again over Battersby Moor.

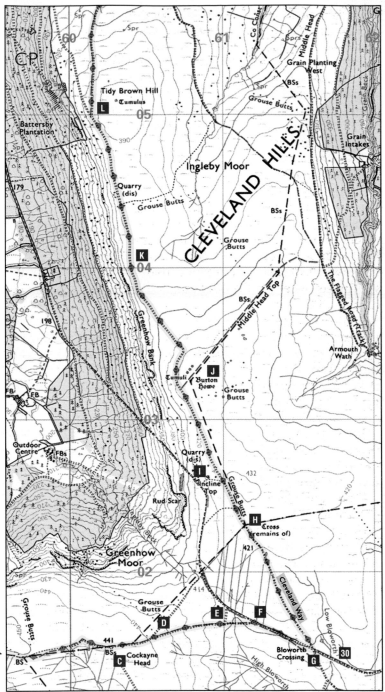

Contours are given in metres
The vertical interval is 10m

79

The track eventually leads through a hand gate and on to the tarmac road **M** where you continue straight ahead. The road itself turns on a sharp bend here leading down into Baysdale. The last farm along the road was built on the site of Baysdale Abbey but there are no remains of the Cistercian nunnery.

The remainder of the Trail to Kildale is on a tarmac surface. At the cattle grid **N** the road turns to drop down from Warren Moor. From the corner northwards, Park Dyke stretches for a mile along the edge of the moor. The dyke, an earth mound and stone wall, is believed to have been part of an enclosure for a medieval deer park.

As the road descends you will see Park Nab **O**, on the right, which provides a few rock climbs for local enthusiasts. On reaching the road junction turn right into the village of Kildale.

Ironstone

In 1861 the soltitude of the moors around Rosedale and Farndale was broken by the invasion of the great iron monster – the railway engine. A railway line had been built from Rosedale, snaking its way round the head of the dales, across the moor to reach the Cleveland escarpment edge above Ingleby. The company which operated the newly discovered ironstone mines in Rosedale selected this moorland route to transport the cargo to the blast furnaces of Teesside and Durham. The Cleveland Way meets the track-bed of this ghostly moorland line at Bloworth Crossing **G**; there cannot be a more isolated spot for a railway crossing in Britain. Railways and ironstone were partners in a 19th-century boom: the railways both created the demand and provided the transport for the exportation of ironstone. In a period of almost 70 years, until it closed in 1929, the Rosedale railway hauled over 10 million tons of ore.

The Cleveland Way touches on ironstone history elsewhere along the Cleveland Hills, in East Cleveland and down the coast. All the evidence of bloomeries, drift mines, track-beds and miners' cottages reveals an industry which existed in the area for almost 2,000 years. Its long history dates from the Iron Age bloomery discovered on Levisham Moor (500 BC) to the closure of the last ironstone mine, North Skelton, in 1964.

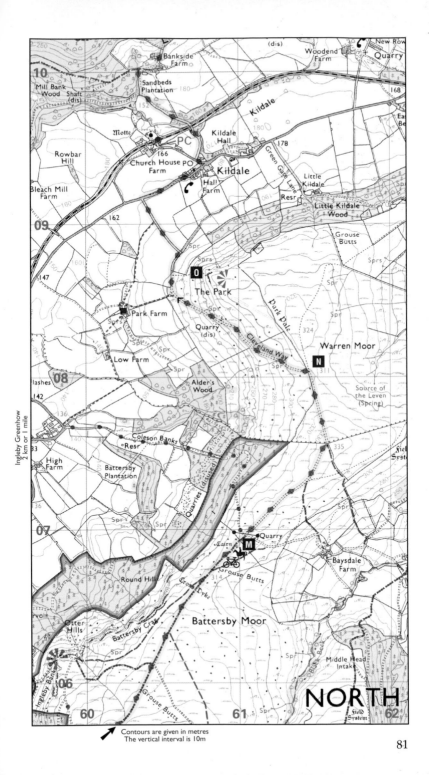

5 Kildale to Saltburn

past Roseberry Topping and through Skelton
14¾ miles (23.75 km)

The early part of this section is dominated by the approach to Roseberry Topping. Once conquered, your reward from the top of this moorland 'Matterhorn' is a sense of achievement and a magnificent panoramic view. Follow the map and directions carefully through Guisborough Woods. The forest paths are somewhat confusing and it is easy to get lost. This is a relatively long and fairly tiring section that ends when you reach the sea at Saltburn.

Proceed through Kildale village and take the first turning on your left which leads to the railway station and church. After some 30 yards (27 metres) take the first turning right down the lane – this is a gated road leading to Guisborough. The road passes under the railway bridge of the Esk Valley Railway **31** and then over the River Leven which flows westwards, eventually to join the River Tees. When the road emerges from the woodland, Kildale church comes into view on the left, perched on the high south bank of the river.

Continue uphill past Bankside Cottage and Bankside Farm, with pleasant views looking back down on to Kildale and eastwards down the Esk Valley.

Go through the farm gate and continue up the road as it climbs steeply through Pale End plantation. At the brow of the hill **A** leave the tarmac road and turn left into the Lonsdale Forest along the forestry road.

A short way along here the route leaves the forestry road **B** and forks off left into the forest, beside a grassy ride. (Do not take the forest path leading towards the hillside edge.) Then it runs along the top edge of some scrub woodland with the forestry plantation continuing on your right.

The path goes along the edge of Coate Moor and eventually emerges from the forest up a short climb on to some heather moor with the plantation still on your right.

Captain Cook's Monument **32** comes into view when you pass through an open break in the stone wall **C** and reach the edge of Easby Moor. The 60-foot (18-metre) column is a fitting monument to one of Yorkshire's greatest sons and is a landmark for many miles around.

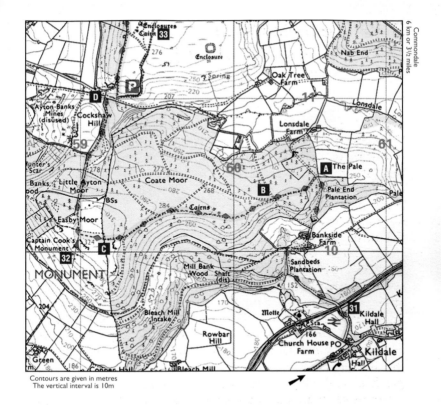

Contours are given in metres
The vertical interval is 10m

A number of paths radiate from the monument; yours lies in a north-north-easterly direction. The need for stone steps and pitching reflects the threat of erosion posed by the large numbers of visitors who visit the monument. The wide path continues down through the forestry plantation which covers Little Ayton Moor.

The path descends Cockshaw Hill through the plantation. Go through the gate **D** at the bottom of the hill and turn right along the road for a few yards. The trail then turns sharply left, directly up the stepped path leading to the top of Great Ayton Moor. When you reach the top, the path continues along level ground alongside a small plantation on the left. There are pleasant views looking south with Captain Cook's Monument (behind you for the first time) on the skyline. The words 'enclosures', 'cairn' and 'field system' on the map **33** (and overleaf) give some clue to the wealth of material of archaeological interest to be found on this area of moor. Excavations have revealed evidence of Iron Age farming activities and a Neolithic burial site.

83

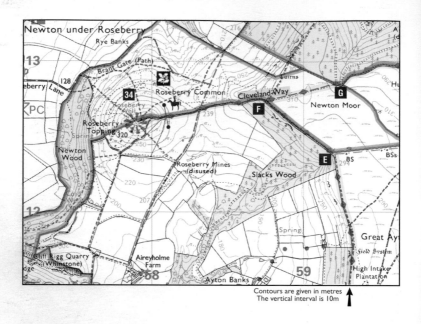

Contours are given in metres
The vertical interval is 10m

A National Trust boundary marker beside the route **E** indicates the Trust's ownership of Roseberry Topping. Also close by at this point there are two ancient boundary stones, and coincidentally these mark the county boundary as we move north out of North Yorkshire into the Borough of Redcar & Cleveland.

At the northern end of Slacks Wood **F** there is a hand gate in the wall ahead. Go through and down to the left, along the obvious track, to climb to the summit of Roseberry Topping **34**. This is the most distinctive peak along the route of the Cleveland Way. The detour may be tiring but the views are exhilarating. From Roseberry Topping return through the hand gate back on to Newton Moor. Take the bridleway which bisects the angle of the boundary walls, leading on to the moor in an easterly direction. Across Newton Moor you reach the corner of a forestry plantation **G**. Go through the hand gate in the forest fence and turn right. Follow the track round the edge of the plantation to the next gate on your right-hand side in the fence. Go through the gate to join the wide track leading up across Hutton Moor. Continue along here for 200 yards (180 metres) then turn left **H** along a narrow green path. The path follows a contour line at first then bends round to the left, leading downhill to meet the corner of a stone wall **I** below Black Nab.

The Trail now follows the stone wall on your left-hand side

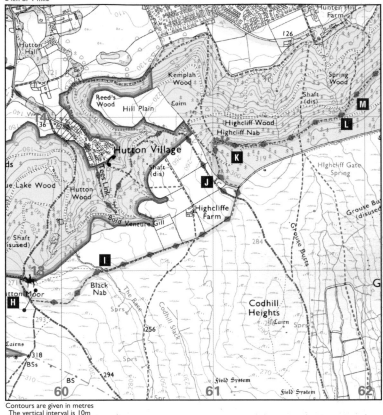

Contours are given in metres
The vertical interval is 10m

across a wide stretch of level ground.

Soon after passing the access to Highcliffe Farm you take a steady uphill route towards the corner of Highcliff Wood. On reaching the plantation, turn left through a hand gate and continue ahead at the edge of the forest. At a break in the forest **J**, turn right uphill to meet a forestry track. Cross over the track and continue up the hill leading to Highcliff Nab.

On emerging from the forest, climb up steeply to the right. From the viewpoint of Highcliff Nab a superb bird's eye view of Guisborough opens out in front of you. From here the Cleveland Way takes you on 2 miles (3.2 km) of route-finding exercise through Guisborough Woods. Continue along the escarpment edge to reach a forestry road **K**. Turn left along this wide road and look for a path branching off left **L** and gently downhill. Take this path; it soon levels out **M** and bears right (another path comes in from the left).

You meet a track which comes sweeping round and down the hillside. At this junction **N** turn right and follow the track as it takes a left bend uphill. The path then levels out.

A forest track comes downhill and meets your path **O**. Continue ahead on the level track and ignore any other routes or public paths for almost a mile. Eventually your path reaches a T-junction **P**. Turn left here downhill to emerge shortly from the forest. The Trail bends right, round the outside of a field.

Leave this track (just before it bends round left) and climb over a stile on the right into the field **Q**. Turn immediately left to cross a small gully and field to reach a stile. Cross the stile and turn left downhill along the track and concrete farm road. At the bottom of the driveway turn right over a stile **R** and follow a narrow enclosed path. Cross over the stile at the end of the enclosed path and turn right through the woodland.

The path climbs up by the edge of the wood to a wide clearing; take the path leading uphill. At the next network of tracks go diagonally uphill at 11 o'clock and over a stile. Continue along a fairly level path. After the next clearing, continue ahead over the metal stile **S**. The path reaches a track where you turn left downhill. Cross the stile at the bottom of the hill and turn left along the old road. Continue along the roadside towards Guisborough, then cross the road and turn right down the old road, over the bridge and past the Fox and Hounds.

Walk past the row of houses and leave the old road on a footpath alongside the fence line of the last house on the right **T**. On reaching a track turn right uphill into the quarry. The Trail is then immediately on your right; cross over the stile and then climb steeply up the steps through the gorse and round the rim of the quarry.

Climb over the stile at the top of the quarry **U** and continue uphill along an enclosed path. This soon levels out and follows the woodland edge to reach a stile at the end of the enclosed path **V**. Cross over the stile and turn right up the edge of the field. The Trail continues through a field gate and uphill along a farm vehicle track, eventually levelling out with a stone wall boundary on your right.

Continue past Airy Hill Farm along the farm access road to join the tarmac road at Skelton Green.

At the road junction **W** in Skelton Green continue ahead along Airy Hill lane to the main road. Cross straight over the road, through the gate and along the enclosed tarmac path

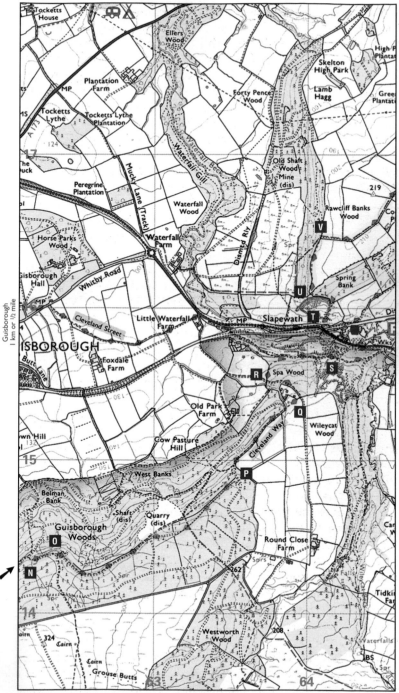

Contours are given in metres
The vertical interval is 10m

Guisborough
I km or 1/2 mile

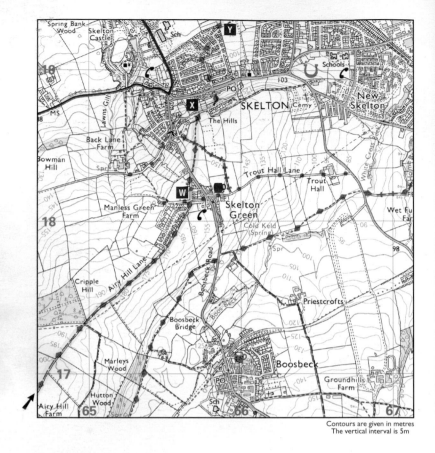

Contours are given in metres
The vertical interval is 5m

through the fields. Continue ahead at the junction with a bridleway. At the end of the path go through a gate and on to some open ground with a view down over Skelton castle. Turn right **X** along the lane for a few yards and then take the steps leading down to the left into the village.

On reaching the main street, cross straight over (there may be a diversion here in the future, due to development) and go downhill along Coniston Road. At the foot of the hill turn right into Ullswater Drive. At the junction with Derwent Road turn left and walk downhill. The road bends right and levels out to enter the field by a gate **Y**. Take the path leading diagonally downhill to the left (not the path straight ahead).

The path is easily defined and continues under the Skelton–Brotton bypass to enter the wood. A winding pathway takes you down through the woodland to reach Skelton Beck. Follow the path downstream a short distance to cross the beck by a

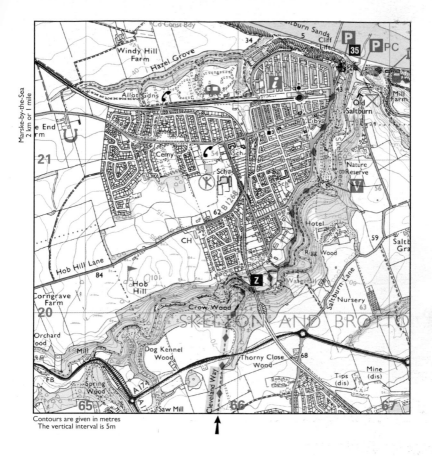

Contours are given in metres
The vertical interval is 5m

footbridge. You pass under the railway viaduct and along a short stretch of enclosed pathway. This is part of the Marske Mill Heritage Trail; the mill ruins are just 150 yards away.

Emerging from the woodland **Z** turn left along the track leading uphill. Towards the top of the lane there is a welcoming seat below a curved stone wall. Turn right at the seat, along a path through the woodland. Keep to the level path avoiding any paths branching off to either side.

All paths lead through the valley down to the sea front of Saltburn-by-the-Sea **35**, but the Cleveland Way takes a path leading uphill above the Valley Gardens to reach the main road.

At the main road turn right and continue along the footpath towards the sea. Take the first road on the right which twists down to the sea front (some steps cut off the bends in the road). From now on the sea will be a constant companion for the next 52 miles (84 km) to Filey.

Esk Valley Railway

One of the few country rail routes to escape the axe of closure is the Esk Valley Railway which runs for 35 miles (56 km) from Middlesbrough to Whitby. The Cleveland Way crosses the line at Kildale **31** and again at its coastal terminus of Whitby. There are ten village stations along this scenic line which keeps close company with the River Esk on its way to the sea. Train time-tables are published in the *Moors Explorer* booklet available free from Tourist Information Centres.

Captain Cook

You will be reminded of this remarkable 18th-century explorer at three locations along the route of the Cleveland Way. Standing high on Easby Moor is the Cook Monument **32** erected in his memory in 1827. Secondly, a plaque on the wall of what is known as Cook's Cottage will be seen in Staithes, the young Cook's first link with the sea. The third location is Whitby where a fine statue of Cook gazes out across the harbour, the scene of his first journey on the sea.

James Cook is Cleveland's most famous son and one of the greatest circumnavigators of the world. He was born in Marton in Cleveland, now part of Middlesbrough, in 1728. His young days were spent on a farm under the shadow of Roseberry Topping and he went to school in Great Ayton. The location of his first job, behind the counter of a local merchant's shop in Staithes, gave him a yearning for the sea. Before long he was off

The monument to Captain Cook on Easby Moor.

to Whitby and signed on as an apprentice on a coalship in 1747. His brilliant career with the Royal Navy began in 1755 and lasted nearly 25 years. He was tragically killed by natives in Hawaii.

Roseberry Topping

The boundary between North Yorkshire and the Borough of Redcar & Cleveland cuts cleanly across the summit **34**. Although it is just over 1,050 feet (320 metres) above sea level its significance is heightened by its separation from the main Cleveland escarpment and also by the dramatic rock face on its western flank. This is Yorkshire's Matterhorn and the nearest you will get to a mountain on the Cleveland Way.

From its solid-rock summit you will have the widest range of views on the whole trail, including your first glimpse of the coast. The climb may be a test of endurance but, if you have allowed sufficient time, the view is not to be missed.

The distinctive peak of Roseberry was bound to attract folk-lore and legend. One story concerns the baby Prince Oswy of Northumbria, taken to Roseberry by his mother to escape an omen of drowning on a certain day – only to die face-down in a hillside spring.

Roseberry Topping was quarried and mined in the past for ironstone and the collapse of its western face, due to subsid-ence, left a steep crag with a peculiar, sharp-pointed end. It is a site of special scientific interest, noted for fossil plant remains.

Saltburn-by-the-Sea

Saltburn **35** comes in two guises – old and new. Little now remains of the original tiny fishing settlement which sheltered in the mouth of Skelton Beck. As the name implies, the com-munity was also involved in panning salt from the North Sea. At the southern end of the promenade is the Ship Inn, famous for its smuggling connections and also where an organised crime syndicate operated in the 18th century under the land-lord, John Andrew.

The new Saltburn was born relatively late, in the 1860s. It was built by the industrialist and entrepreneur Henry Pease with all the zeal the Victorians poured on their new discovery – seaside resorts. Hence the railway station, Zetland Hotel, cliff railway, pier, and grid-like street pattern with houses built in the light-coloured bricks from Pease's works in County Durham.

6 Saltburn to Sandsend

through Staithes and Runswick
17½ miles (28 km)

An inspiring start from Saltburn takes you up to Hunt Cliff and along a section of dramatic cliffs to the highest point on the east coast of England at Rock Cliff near Boulby. The route takes you down to sea level on three occasions and through the picturesque villages of Staithes and Runswick.

The A174 winds down from Saltburn town to the sea front and crosses Skelton Beck. The local fishing boats are beached on the shore along with their salt-worn tractors. Follow the main road along the sea front to the Ship Inn.

Walk along the footpath past the Ship Inn and car park, then immediately turn left **A** up the steep and stepped hillside (do not use the tarmac footpath). On reaching the top the path follows the cliff edge. This is a fine place to look back westward for your first cliffland view of the coast and Saltburn.

The cliff-edge path is unfenced alongside rolling farmland with what seem endless fields. On reaching the first fence the path keeps to the inland side. Seabirds wheeling over the coastal cliffs will now become a common sight and the coastal views just here have greater interest than the hedgeless prairie on the right.

The way rises gently up to Hunt Cliff and you will pass a plaque commemorating the site of the Hunt Cliff Roman signal station **36**. The coastline from Saltburn to Scalby Ness was defined as a Heritage Coast in 1974 and the plaque was erected by the authorities responsible for the North Yorkshire and Cleveland Heritage Coast.

At the start of a short enclosed section there is a warning about the danger of sheer cliffs; this is a warning which applies many times along this coastal walk. The path continues near the railway track for some time. This railway **37** (see map on page 94) is now used solely as a mineral line serving the Boulby potash mine, further along the way. Extra caution is needed in wet weather as a section of the path, close to the cliff edge, can be quite muddy. To the right are the remains of the Huntcliff mine, with the Guibal Fan House on the far side of the railway line. The Fan was used to ventilate the mine, which was in production from 1872 to 1906.

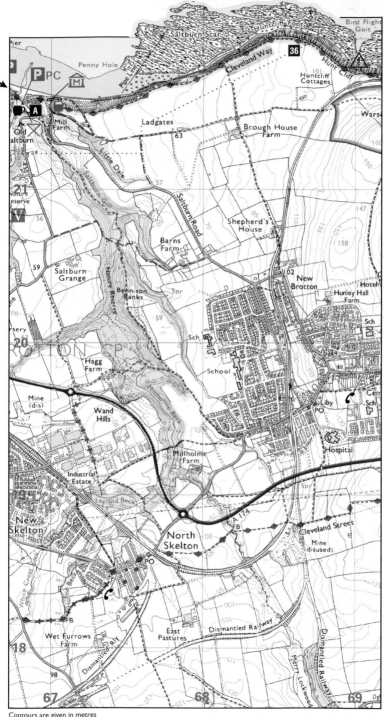

Contours are given in metres
The vertical interval is 5m

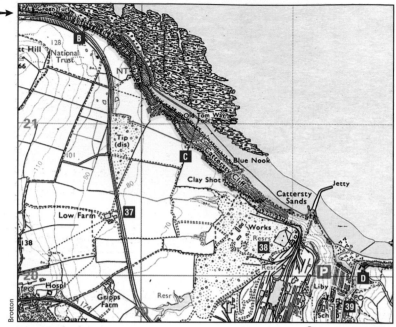

Contours are given in metres
The vertical interval is 10m

The path leaves the company of the railway track (the line continues its mighty sweep around Warsett Hill) and turns left **B** along the fence line to rejoin the cliff edge. A line of sandy beach (Cattersty Sands) and a jetty come into view ahead. The prairie landscape continues inland with the old hedge lines indicated by small grass banks and the odd wind-worn hawthorn bush. At the end of a short unenclosed section **C** go left of the fence line and the path then descends the fairly steep hill with the aid of some steps down to the beach. The slap waste from the now demolished blast furnaces of the Skinningrove Ironworks **38** spills over the hillside. The walk through the soft, dry sand dune is slow going and leads to the Skinningrove jetty. Go through the underpass and continue ahead. The surfaced path leads to the village of Skinningrove **39** where you turn left along Marine Terrace.

Skinningrove was transformed from a small fishing village after the discovery of local ironstone and houses were built to accommodate the miners and blast-furnacemen. At the end of the terrace of houses continue ahead, then turn left over the Kilton Beck Bridge. Fishing boats and tractors are parked on the roadside here.

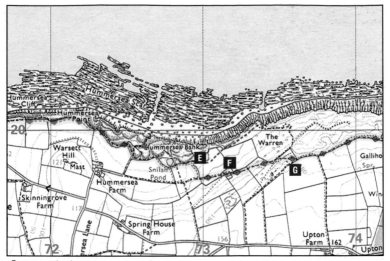

Contours are given in metres
The vertical interval is 10m

The road sweeps round **D**, and you take the steep steps to the top of the hill. Catch your breath at the top and look back on the village, the modern steelworks and along the coast to the jetty and beyond.

The path along Hummersea Cliff eventually reaches a fence line, where another path leads down to Hummersea Beach. The Cleveland Way turns right here **E** inland along the slight uphill track. At the next T-junction, turn left along the farm road leading to an isolated farmhouse **F**.

Continue past the front of the house and you will see a stile to the right of the garage/stable building. Cross that stile, and shortly after it the next stile, to continue ahead gently uphill through the field. The route leads to a bracken-covered hillside and climbs steadily uphill to the top, where you regain the cliff top **G** by the stone wall (do not descend alongside the quarry).

As the path sweeps round Gallihowe you re-enter the North York Moors National Park. Stretching below you for the next mile or so are extensive remains of the alum workings along this part of the coast. The workings below Gallihowe were known as the Loftus (or Lingberry) Alum Quarries and further on were the Boulby Alum Quarries. Both quarries operated for over 200 years from the mid-17th century to the mid-19th century. An interpretive plaque provided by the Heritage Coast authorities stands above a good view of the Boulby Alum Quarries and works. Here, above Rock Cliff **40**, you are standing on the

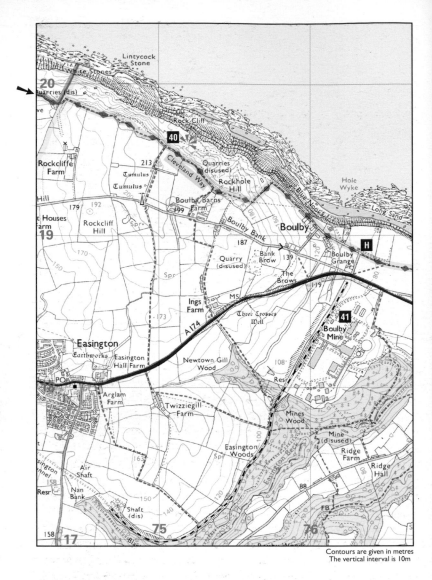

highest cliff on the east coast of England, 666 feet (203 metres) above sea level.

When Boulby comes into view the route descends the hillside through the bracken and heather to a boundary wall, then drops steeply alongside the wall towards the coastal cliffs. The path then turns right along the fence line leading to the row of cottages.

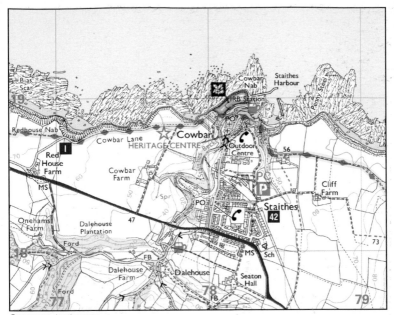

Contours are given in metres
The vertical interval is 10m

Continue ahead down the road to the bottom of the hill. On the way down, Boulby Potash Mine **41** comes into view. The deepest mining shaft in England operates at the Boulby potash mine and was completed in 1973. The mineral is mined at a depth of about 4,000 feet (1,220 metres) and is a prime source of agricultural fertiliser. Leave the road as it turns sharp right **H** and continue ahead across the farm access road and over a stile to an enclosed section of path. For the first time since Saltburn you will see and hear traffic on a main road. Continue across open fields, where the path marks a field boundary.

The field path joins the road **I** leading along Cowbar Lane to Cowbar and Staithes **42**. The steep drop from Cowbar presents a dramatic view over Staithes Beck. The beck is a local government boundary and you leave the Borough of Redcar & Cleveland to rejoin North Yorkshire. Cross the footbridge and at the main street turn left for the sea front. Just past the Cod and Lobster Inn, turn right up Church Street. Note the plaque on the cottage recording Captain Cook's apprenticeship in Staithes.

At the top of the lane continue up the track and take the left fork up past the farm buildings. A level walk through fields leads you to a short uphill stretch to the corner of a field where the coastal cliffs are joined once again. Half a mile (800 metres) further on you

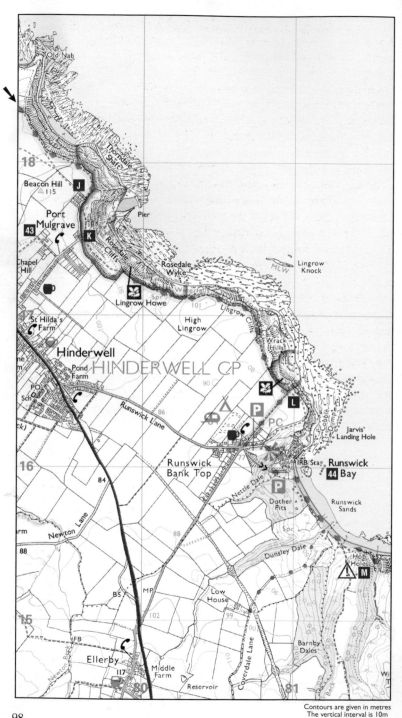

Old Nab

Thorndale Shaft

18

Beacon Hill
△115 **J**

Port
Mulgrave
43

K

Rosedale
Cliffs

Pier

Rosedale
Wyke

Lingrow
Knock

MLW

Chapel
Hill

Lingrow Howe

Waterfall
Spring

101

Lingrow Cliffs

Rosedale
Wyke

St Hilda's
Farm

17

High
Lingrow

100

Wrack
Hills

Hinderwell

Pond
Farm

HINDERWELL CP

98

90

86

08

L

PO
Sch

Runswick Lane

△

P

PC

Cobble
Dump

Jarvis'
Landing Hole

16

Runswick
Bank Top

84

Nettle Dale

IRB Stas

Runswick
44 Bay

P

Dother
Pits

Runswick
Sands

Newton Lane

88

Spa

88

Dunsley Dale

Hob
Holes

⚠ **M**

BS

MP

Low
House

99

00

06

15

102

FB

Ellerby

110

Coverdale Lane

Barnby
Dales

Beck

117

Middle
Farm

80

Reservoir

81

Wi

Newton Beck

Contours are given in metres
The vertical interval is 10m

reach Port Mulgrave **43** where the route turns away from the cliffs **J** and towards the line of houses along the field edge to reach a tarmac lane. Continue along the lane; you will have a good view down on to the tiny harbour and jetty.

On reaching the next row of houses, turn off left **K** along a path, and continue ahead with the fence on your right. The path arcs round to meet the cliffs again and then along the edge of an open field. The path around Lingrow Cliffs and Wrack Hills is followed easily.

Along the cliff path, the fence line ends in a stile **L**; turn right over the stile. The pond in the corner (on private land) is a rare sight along the walk. It is man-made, a remnant from the iron-stone industry and is a habitat for newts. A short enclosed section of path emerges at Runswick Bank Top beside the hotel. Turn left and follow the old road down into Runswick Bay **44**.

Turn right along the slipway to the beach, turn right and then walk along the sands for half a mile, going past the wooden buildings of the Runswick Bay Sailing Club. The easily eroded shale is exposed along the cliffs, and the caves along the beach are known as Hob Holes – a place where legend has it that whooping cough could be cured by the resident hob-goblin. If the tide is in, wait for it to recede. There is no alternative.

A small beck comes out of a deep break in the cliffs **M**. Walk up alongside the beck (the shales are dangerously slippery in wet weather) to cross a footbridge and climb steeply up the hillside to High Cliff and the coastal path.

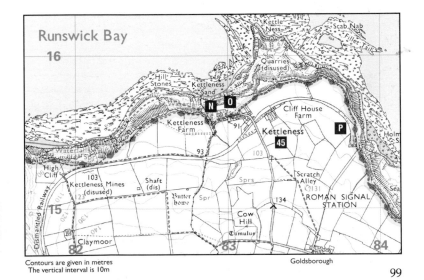

Contours are given in metres
The vertical interval is 10m

Goldsborough

Approaching Kettleness **45** the path turns inland alongside a narrow gully **N**. At the farm track turn left over the stile and continue on the track, past the house, and go straight ahead through the farmyard between the buildings. (This part of the route may be diverted in the future.) On reaching the tarmac road turn off left **O** along a track, through a gate and keep to the left-hand track nearest the coast. The path sweeps round above Kettleness on the coastal side of two large fields to meet the track-bed of the disused railway **P**. After a few yards leave the rail track (it disappears into an old overgrown tunnel entrance), up a slight rise with the fence line on your left. A succession of stiles interrupts the easily followed trail along the cliffs.

The trail keeps close to the coastal cliffs until you approach Deepgrove Wyke **Q**. Take care with a very steep descent through trees. At the bottom you rejoin the old railway track.

This is the easiest part of the day's walk. The level track-bed takes you through the extensive spoil heaps of the former Sandsend Alum Quarries. Leave the track-bed **R** by the steps down into Sandsend car park.

Fishing

Passing through the smaller coastal settlements along the Cleveland Way you may be conscious of the particular style of gaily-painted fishing boats exhibited in the harbours or on the beaches. This is the Yorkshire coble, pronounced 'cobble'. The boats are beached up on the shore, usually with tractors in attendance. Not exclusive to Yorkshire, cobles have a pedigree stretching back to the Vikings; the basic design which reflects the Viking long-boat is relatively unchanged. Heavy in relation to their size, these sturdy cobles can cut through the harsh North Sea with their sharp, steep bows and can be beach-landed due to their flat-bottomed construction. Sail-powered cobles kept whole families busy in the fishing business, from baiting to trading, during the 18th and 19th centuries.

The march of progress stole a living from the coastal communities. The invention of the steam engine and the construction of large trawlers steaming out of the bigger ports put paid to their way of life by the 1920s. Revival has come in the form of larger cobles, hauled out to sea by tractors, and modern fishing gear and such aids as echo-sounders. The herring has declined in number and now the search is on for crab, lobster, cod, plaice and haddock.

Contours are given in metres
The vertical interval is 10m

Smuggling

Like most crimes, smuggling was profit-motivated. When the government of the day imposed sufficiently high taxes to make the risks worthwhile, smuggling became a major activity in the communities along the Yorkshire coast. For a period of around 150 years (1700–1850) a profitable living could be made from the illegal trade in tea, spirits, salt and silk. The tax on tea, for example, was unbelievably high. Tea could be bought in Holland for 7d (pre-decimal pence) a pound, and yet cost between 20 and 60 times as much in England, depending on its quality and place of origin. It is not surprising, therefore, that three-quarters of the tea drunk annually in England was illegally imported.

The many inlets along the cliffed coastline and the isolated fishing villages of Staithes, Runswick and Robin Hood's Bay made good landing places for bootleg cargo. Revenue men and soldiers were also kept busy in the desperate and sometimes bloody battle against the smugglers in Saltburn, Whitby and Scarborough.

One of the busiest smuggling communities was that of Robin Hood's Bay. Tales abound of the ruthless wit and daring of the smugglers against the customs men in the village. Close-packed houses with secret connecting doors were said to allow a roll of silk to pass from the bottom of the village to the top without ever seeing daylight. Mayhem was so common in the village that a troop of dragoons was stationed there permanently until 1830.

Seabirds

For the non-specialist, there are numerous seabirds along the cliffs and beaches, not all of which are easy to distinguish. Even if you cannot identify them you certainly cannot avoid their cacophony of calls resounding from the cliff-ledge nesting sites.

As you walk along the cliff edge your nearest air-borne companion will most often be the fulmar. It loves to ride the currents, gliding majestically with wings kept rigid as it skirts the cliff face. The fulmar flies close enough for you to be able to observe the two short-tubed nostrils attached to its bill.

There are many fine nesting sites along the cliffed coastline, such as Hunt Cliff near Saltburn and Hundale Point north of Scarborough, with mixed colonies of seabirds. The commonest of the larger gulls is the herring gull. Equally at home on coastal cliffs, house roofs, harbour walls and fishing boats, this scavenger is not at all shy of human activities. The colour of the legs, eyes, bill and back are important identification features of gulls. The herring gull is identified by a combination of pink legs, pale yellow eyes, yellow bill and light grey back.

Despite its name, the common gull is not in fact our commonest gull. The yellow-green legs and dark eyes of this smaller and more delicate-looking gull distinguish it from the herring gull.

Cormorants and shags are two large black birds of the coastal cliffs, which may be seen diving after fish or simply standing on a rocky perch with wings outspread to dry their feathers. The birds are quite similar, and their long necks and beaks are obvious as they swim with a characteristic head-up posture. The cormorant is distinguished by its white face patch.

Filey Brigg is a popular location for bird watching, particularly during the spring and autumn migrations. The Arctic tern does not breed along this coast but only passes through, twice yearly, between its breeding ground (Northumberland to the Arctic) and its winter quarters (Antarctica). These journeys make it the most travelled bird in the world. Almost identical in appearance is the common tern, a summer visitor to Britain which nests along the Heritage Coast. The graceful lines of these terns are a delight to observe as they hover and dive into the sea for small fish.

The Romans

One of the factors that contributed to the success of the Roman occupation of Britain was the development of a road network radiating from regional fortresses. The Romans arrived in North Yorkshire around AD 70 and built garrison towns at York and Malton. One of the roads from Malton led across the desolate moors to a terminus on the coast. No doubt this road became valuable much later, in the 4th century, for transporting soldiers in a struggle against Saxon raiders from across the North Sea. The cliffed coastline played its part in providing strategic headlands where the Romans erected fortified lookout posts or signal stations.

The Cleveland Way passes the site of the signal stations positioned at Hunt Cliff **36**, Goldsborough, Ravenscar, Scarborough and Filey. After 15 centuries of change and coastal erosion the only remains are a few bumps in a Goldsborough field and some foundations at the cliff edge of Scarborough Castle grounds.

Staithes with its houses huddled together and a fleet of cobles in the beck.

105

Heritage Coast

From Saltburn to Scalby Ness, near Scarborough, the Cleveland Way follows a stretch of exceptionally attractive coastline defined as a Heritage Coast. The official title of the 36-mile (58-km) coastline is the North Yorkshire and Cleveland Heritage Coast. It is just one of a number of particularly beautiful coastline stretches which were selected in the 1970s by the Countryside Commission and defined as Heritage Coasts. The aims are to ensure the protection of the environment and to make provision for public enjoyment of the coastline while safeguarding the interests of local people. Much of this coastline therefore enjoys a dual protection as it lies within the North York Moors National Park.

A major emphasis has been placed on the protection of this coastline, and a consortium of five planning authorities form the steering group responsible for its policies and administration. The day-to-day practical and administrative duties are the responsibility of the Heritage Coast Ranger, who deals with the needs and interests of landowners, residents and visitors. Literature on the Heritage Coast and details of the guided walks programme are available from Tourist Information Centres and the Heritage Coast Ranger (see page 142).

Skinningrove

Geology has much to answer for. The random deposition of certain rocks is a factor in determining the geographical distribution of a country's population and has often prompted the rise of whole new towns. In the case of Skinningrove **39** the discovery of ironstone in 1847 transformed a quiet fishing village into unadorned rows of terrace houses built to accommodate the influx of miners and blast-furnace workers. The terrace houses have been rebuilt with modern amenities and Kilton Beck is somewhat less discoloured by iron oxides. The hillside is dotted with pigeon lofts – a favourite local pastime – and cobles still go out from the beach.

The British Steel works **38** at Skinningrove are the last surviving link along the Cleveland Way with an activity that dominated the Cleveland industrial scene during the last half of the 19th century and initiated the growth of Middlesbrough from a tiny hamlet to a city complex. Although it is still referred to as the Skinningrove Ironworks it no longer processes local ironstone and is reduced from its former extent and activity. A fairly rich seam of iron ore was discovered at Skinningrove in 1847 and the mines played an early part in Cleveland's 'iron rush' of the 1850s. There is a museum at the former Loftus iron-stone mine at the western end of the village. It is one of the places to visit on an industrial trail through Skinningrove.

Staithes

Only a handful of villages have direct access to the sea along the Cleveland Way from Saltburn to Filey. The picturesque village of Staithes **42** must be one of the most photographed of these harbour villages. The view over the tiny inlet of Staithes Beck with the dramatic backdrop of Cowbar Nab presents an undeniably charming scene. There is little elbow-room in the old part of the village, where narrow alleyways and steep steps provide occasional access between the close-knit cottages. On a summer's day the beautiful setting belies the true nature of the existence lived out by generations of fisher folk at this remote inlet. Ruthless storms have taken their toll of men's lives, boats and property from the village. The seafront shop where the young James Cook served his apprenticeship was demolished by the sea in the 18th century. As you walk safely past the Cod and Lobster Inn you might note that three times it has suc-cumbed to the ravages of the North Sea. On the last occasion, in 1953, the inn was severely damaged. Staithes proudly retains its character of individuality and a small inshore fleet of cobles still sets out from the shelter of its harbour.

Port Mulgrave

The derelict state of the miniature harbour at Port Mulgrave **43** makes a forlorn sight. This was never a fishing port; it owes its existence to the 19th-century boom in ironstone mining. It was decided to transport the iron ore from the Grinkle mines, 3 miles (5 km) inland, by a series of tunnels to the coast. The harbour at Port Mulgrave was built where the tunnel (now sealed) emerged at the foot of the cliffs. The tiny harbour was kept busy from 1874 to 1916 but when the mines closed so did the com-mercial life of the harbour.

Runswick

The soft and slippery Jurassic shales which outcrop along the coast are much in evidence at Runswick Bay **44**. Their instability caused a landslip in 1682 and the village had to be rebuilt. The attractive red-roofed houses cling to the hillside at the northern end of the wide bay with its fine stretch of sandy beach. Numerous paths wind between the houses and their attractive gardens. A few fishing cobles and pleasure craft add to Runswick's seafaring aspect.

Kettleness

As if to warn us a second time about coastal instability, we find that the original village of Kettleness **45** suffered the same disastrous fate as neighbouring Runswick Bay. During one night in 1829 the cliff slipped gently into the sea. The entire village went with it and the inhabitants took refuge on an alum ship standing offshore. The extensive working of alum which resumed again after the disaster is responsible for the obvious demolition of half the nab at Kettleness Point. Quarrying in 1857 exposed the fossils of reptiles from the Jurassic era and these are now exhibited in the Pannett Park Museum in Whitby.

Rock cliff near Boulby, the highest point on the East Coast of England.

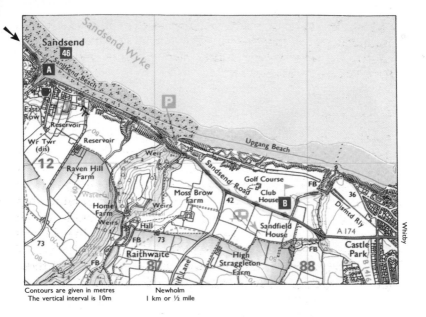

Contours are given in metres
The vertical interval is 10m

Newholm
1 km or ½ mile

7 Sandsend to Robin Hood's Bay

through Whitby
10 miles (16.25 km)

The greatest interest in this section lies in Whitby and Robin Hood's Bay, separated by an easy clifftop walk. The River Esk comes down to the sea at Whitby and its fine harbour. The growth of this town was based on an early prosperity, from seafaring. An air of mystery surrounds Robin Hood's Bay and its isolation once suited the supply of contraband goods.

As its name implies, Sandsend **46** lies at the end of the stretch of sandy beach leading to Whitby, a distance of some 2 miles (3.2 km). Your route is along the roadside footpath which leaves the car park and crosses Sandsend Beck, the first of the two becks here. Alternatively, if the tide is out you might choose to walk along the beach, thus avoiding the traffic.

Sandsend comprises two communities. The south-easterly one is East Row through which you pass as the road winds round and over East Row Beck **A**. The roadside footpath continues along the sea front towards Whitby for the next mile or so. The road climbs gently uphill and is deflected from the coast by the golf course. Look for a track on your left **B** opposite a caravan park; this takes you under a high-level footbridge over the gully. Do not descend to the beach but walk up to the right to

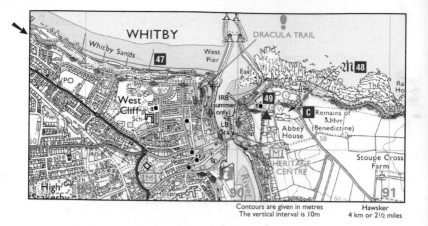

Contours are given in metres
The vertical interval is 10m

Hawsker
4 km or 2½ miles

reach the cliff edge. The Trail follows the cliff edge into Whitby, along a tarmac path. Colourful beach huts below, with the west pier and abbey beyond, are your first views of Whitby **47**.

Overlooking the harbour at the mouth of the River Esk there is a statue of Captain Cook. Whitby was once the greatest whaling port in the country. The jawbones of a whale make an apt archway over your path leading down to the hairpin bend in the road (the Khyber Pass). Continue downhill to the harbour front and along the quayside, with the fish market on one side and the amusement arcades on the other.

Cross over the swing bridge (it swings open during high water to allow the passage of large vessels between the lower and upper harbours) and turn left along the narrow pedestrian lane (Sandgate). Some of the shops sell ornaments and jewellery made from Whitby jet. Fossils are displayed in one of the windows, including ammonites, which are a distinctive feature of the Jurassic rocks of the area.

On reaching the small market square turn right past the Town Hall to join Church Street (the town's oldest street). Turn left here and continue into Henrietta Street at the bottom of the Church Stairs – 199 steps dating from 1370. As you climb up the steps you will see the cobbled road on the right (Donkey Road): an old route out of Whitby past the Abbey Gatehouse.

At the top of the steps is Caedmon's Cross; he was a lay brother at Whitby Abbey **48** in the 7th century. Nearby is St Mary's Church **49** with an interior worth visiting.

The churchyard path leads to the car park where there is access to the ruins of the abbey. The Cleveland Way runs along the perimeter wall of the abbey, past the entrance to the

Coastguard Operation Room and BBC mast (the route may be diverted in the future). Take the last entrance **C** on the left into Abbey Farm, through the gate and in front of the house. The track continues to the right of the farm building and straight ahead through the field to reach the cliff edge. Turn right over the stile and follow the path all the way to Saltwick Holiday Park. Seabirds are your companions as you view Saltwick Nab (a National Trust property) **D** thrusting out into the North Sea.

A stony path eventually leads to the tarmac road in the holiday village. Turn left and follow the road past the shop and reception area. As you exit from the park you turn off left along the cliff line once again.

Contours are given in metres
The vertical interval is 10m

Hawsker
1 km or ½ mile

The Trail passes in front of the former Fog Signal Station and turns right at the end of the next field E to the top corner by the lighthouse. Cross over the access road and go left along the path on the outside of the lighthouse perimeter wall. The path crosses a field and runs parallel to the cliff edge up to a high point on the cliff.

The route is easily followed to Robin Hood's Bay, dipping down to a number of streams along the way. Take care in wet weather as the path on the cliff top can be very muddy and slippery.

The point at which the footpath comes down the side of Oakham Beck to Maw Wyke Hole F is where the Coast to Coast path reaches the North Sea after 187 miles (300 km) from St Bees in Cumbria.

The route continues around North Cheek (Ness Point) leading into Robin Hood's Bay 50. The sweep of the bay comes into view looking across to South Cheek near Ravenscar, but the village remains hidden. Eventually you turn left along a path enclosed by hawthorns to emerge on to a path in front of the houses. Continue ahead along the street (Mount Pleasant North) and turn left at the junction with the main road through the village.

The Cleveland Way takes you along the main street to a fine view across the bay from the car park edge and down the steep bank into the old part of the village.

Sandsend

If you use Sandsend car park as your viewing platform and turn your back on Sandsend Ness, the classic picture postcard is revealed – sandy beach, sea-worn breakwaters, stream escaping to the sea along an alleyway strewn with boulders, backcloth of scrub-covered cliff, assorted cottages just above sea level, crabpot markers and fishing boats in a gentle curving bay. Renowned for its long sandy beach, Sandsend 46, as its name implies, is quite simply the settlement at the end of Whitby sands. It has a busy tourist season, for in addition to its attractive natural features it lies on the main coast road from Teesside to Whitby.

The village is in actual fact an amalgamation of two separate settlements, Sandsend and East Row. They grew originally round the two separate becks descending either side of the hump-backed Sandsend Rigg. Rows of cottages were built to

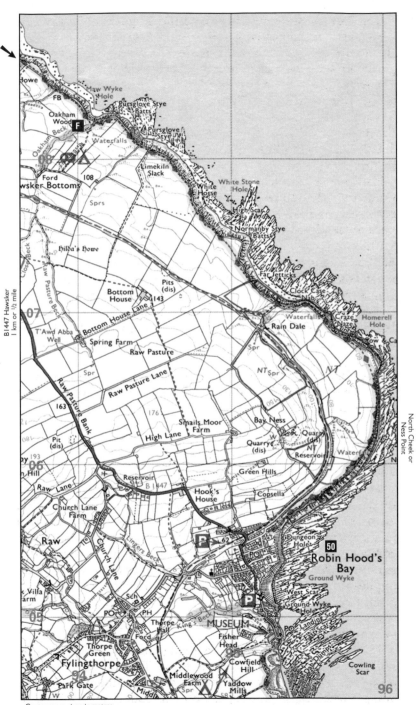

Contours are given in metres
The vertical interval is 10m

B 1447 Hawsker
1 km or ½ mile

North Cheek or
Ness Point

Howe
FB
Maw Wyke
Hole
Oakham
Wood
Pursglove Stye
Batts
Oakham Beck
F
Pursglove
Stye
Waterfalls
Limekiln
Slack
White
Hosse
White Stone
Hole
08
Ford
Hwsker Bottoms
108
Sprs
High Scar
Normanby Stye
Batts
Hilda's Howe
Far Jetticks
Close Beck
Raw Pasture Beck
Pits
(dis)
Bottom
House
143
Clock Case
Nab
07
T'Awd Abba
Well
Bottom House Lane
Spring Farm
Raw Pasture
Waterfalls
Rain Dale
Craze
Nazes
Homerell
Hole
Spr
Cow Ca
Raw Pasture Lane
NT Spr
NT
Spr
163
176
Smails Moor
Farm
Bay Ness
Quarry
(dis)
Pit
(dis)
High Lane
Quarry
(dis)
W
NT
Reservoir
Waterfa
06
Hill
193
Raw Lane
Reservoir
B 1447
Green Hills
Copsella
N
Church Lane
Farm
Hook's
House
Robin Hood's
Bay
50
Raw
Villa
arm
Church Lane
Lingers Beck
P
62
Dungeon
Hole
Ground Wyke
West Scar
Ground Wyke
Hole
05
Sch
PO
PH
Thorpe
Hall
Ford
King's Beck
P
MUSEUM
Fisher
Head
Pon
Landing Scar
Cowling
Scar
Thorpe
Green
Fylingthorpe
94
Park Gate
Middlewood
Farm
Spr
Middl
Yaddow
Mills
Cowfield
Hill
96

house the workers from the alum quarries in Mulgrave Woods and Sandsend Ness. The massive shale waste tips bear silent witness to an industry which continued with variable prosperity for over 250 years, finally closing here in 1867.

The railway came to Sandsend in 1855 and brought increased access and prosperity. The 19th- and 20th-century development along the sea front eventually connected the two communities of Sandsend and East Row. The railway line was closed in 1958 and the two enormous viaducts which crossed the becks were dismantled.

Whitby

The history of Whitby's fame and fortune is inevitably linked with the sea. Surrounded by moorland on three sides, the North Sea was its only possible salvation. Its landward isolation was not broken until the coming of the railways, beginning in 1836 when George Stephenson built a horse-drawn rail line from Whitby to Pickering.

Whitby offers a taste of the past, as far back as the 13th-century ruins of Whitby Abbey **48**. The abbey and the harbour are the two magnets which almost immediately hold one's gaze. The quaint narrow streets close to the harbour are lined with small cottages huddled together under a canopy of red roofs. An impetus to the early importance of Whitby was given in the 7th century when St Hilda chose an imposing site on the east cliff on which to build the first abbey. Apart from its establishment as a religious centre, life in the town has always been entwined with fishing and shipping. The period of Whitby's greatest fame and prosperity was from the mid-18th to mid-19th century. This 100-year period (1750–1850) roughly covers the heydays of whaling, shipbuilding and also of the jet trade (see page 71).

The Cleveland Way passes under the whalebone arch erected on the west cliff overlooking the harbour. Many of Whitby's sons lost their lives at sea in the perilous days of sailing ships and no occupation was so hazardous as that of a whaler. For the chance of a high reward, men put their lives at risk from starvation, drowning, disease and serious injury. The first Whitby whaling ships set sail for Greenland in the early 1750s, and for 80 years ships returned each summer. The Greenland right whale was prized for its blubber which was made into oil for lighting, and also for its whalebone used for ladies' dress hoops and corsets. Gas lamps then replaced oil lamps and

The Cleveland Way follows the 199 steps of Church Stairs with a view of Whitby harbour from the top.

Fishing, whaling and shipbuilding have all contributed to Whitby's fame and fortune.

Whitby's whaling bonanza ended in 1837. The exploits of the most famous whaling captains, the William Scoresbys, father and son, are recorded in the Pannett Park Museum in Whitby.

Whitby's shipbuilding industry was already established when the young James Cook, aged 19, served on his first ship out of the harbour in 1747. It says much for the reputation of local craftsmanship that on his voyages of discovery (1768–79) all four of Cook's famous ships – *Endeavour, Resolution, Adventure* and *Discovery* – were Whitby-built.

The gaunt ruins of Whitby Abbey **48** make a dramatic sky-line feature on the cliff top above Whitby. The fame of the abbey was assured in the 7th century through St Hilda, Caedmon and the Synod of Whitby. St Hilda was the first abbess of this 'mixed' monastery (for men and women) founded in AD 657. Hilda encouraged the remarkable talent of Caedmon whose overnight vision inspired him to sing his 'Song of Creation', the first-ever Christian verse in English. The Synod of Whitby in AD 664 was a momentous meeting between the Celtic and Roman traditions of the Christian Church when, among other things, the method for determining the date of Easter was agreed. St Hilda's abbey was destroyed in the 9th century by invading Vikings.

A second abbey was established on the same clifftop site in 1078 and the ruins we see today date largely from the 12th to 15th centuries.

The 12th-century Church of St Mary **49** was built to provide a place of worship for the lay people who worked for the abbey. The interior contains some interesting items, including a three-decker pulpit, galleries, a special pew for the lord of the manor and a 'ship's deck' roof. The latter was built in 1819 with sky-lights and side lights installed by ship's carpenters exactly as they would be on board ship.

8 Robin Hood's Bay to Scarborough

via Ravenscar
13½ miles (22 km)

Small inlets along the Yorkshire coast are often referred to as 'wykes'. There are three steep descents and corresponding climbs along this section where the sea interrupts the clifftop walk. The route up to the breezy cliffs of Ravenscar is punctuated by the two steep inlets of Boggle Hole and Stoupe Beck which take you down to beach level. An even steeper descent reveals the secret hideaway of Hayburn Wyke.

In Robin Hood's Bay go towards the bottom of the road and with the sea in sight, take the second narrow street on the right (Albion Street). At the end of the houses, turn left up Flagstaff Steps, noting the inscription concerning an ancient right of way on the house wall at the bottom of the steps. The climb up the steps is rewarded by a closer view of the bay over to Ravenscar.

Continue up the boardwalk steps at the edge of the coastal slope. The glacial clay covering the cliff slopes is revealed here. The clays are easily eroded by the sea and the coastal edge is particularly unstable and always liable to slumping. If the tide is out you will see the concentric circles of rock ledges called 'scars'. They circle the centre point of an eroded dome out in the bay like the chopped-off top of an onion.

There is a steep descent to Boggle Hole and the youth hostel where you cross Mill Beck by a footbridge. Turn right up the road for a short distance and then take off left, uphill to the cliff path. The Trail descends once again to sea level at Stoupe Beck where there is a footbridge and a steep track up past Stoupe Bank Farm. Continue along the road and just before Stoupebrow Cottage Farm the Trail turns left **A** over a stile to return to the cliff top.

On approaching Ravenscar **51** a drainage ravine turns the Trail away from the cliff top **B** to join a farm access road **C**. Part way up the hill take the first path **D** on the right, lined with gorse and broom. A steady climb takes you past the shale waste tips of the old Ravenscar Alum Works. The path bears left as it levels out. Along a short rise, fork left alongside the fence line, eventually to join a vehicle track laid with bricks from the former Ravenscar Brick Works. The quarries and a 1-mile (1.6-km) stretch of coastal cliff at Ravenscar are owned by the National Trust, whose shop is on your left just as you reach the road into the village.

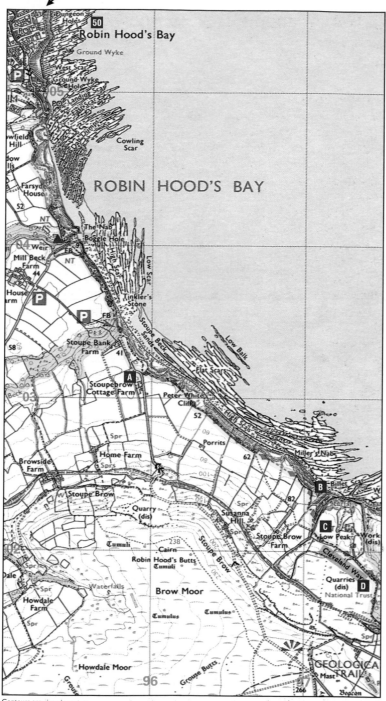

Contours are given in metres
The vertical interval is 10m

119

Contours are given in metres
The vertical interval is 10m

The Raven Hall Hotel welcomes walkers (use the bar entrance) and there are public toilets a short distance along the road south out of the village. The headland at Ravenscar was the site of another Roman signal station. There were ambitious plans to build a seaside holiday resort at Ravenscar in the 1890s but the venture failed – hence the reference to 'a town that never was' (*see page 126*).

Your route continues past the driveway entrance to the hotel and along Station Road for 100 yards (90 metres). Take the first track **E** on the left leading down to the cliff top and turn right along the coast path. You will see on your right that Station Square progressed as far as a terrace of tall houses on one side only. The path passes the Coastguard Lookout Station **F**. The coastline becomes less austere at Beast Cliff, where the slopes are clothed in gorse and scrub woodland.

Petard Point
52
124
Rigg Hall
Farm
East Side
Farm
109
Plane Tree
Cottages
72
Whitehouse
Farm
Herbert Hole
Spr
Whitestone
Red House
Farm
Cleveland Way
Nab End
108
97
Moor
Lodge
Hotel
Hayburn Wyke
(Nature Reserve)
Mean High Water
Mean Low Water
Little Cliff
Tindall Point
NT
Newlands
Dale
112
Iron Scar
159
131
120
The
Hulleys
Caywood
Plantation
Cloughton Newlands
Farm
Rodger
Trod
96
Cloughton Newlands
100
144
Greystone Farm
Holm Slack
MS
82
Sycarham
Farm
102
112
01
Little Moor
100
Salt Pans
Cober
Cloughton
Wyke
Dismantled Railway

A171 Cloughton   Contours are given in metres
1 km or ½ mile   The vertical interval is 10m

121

The coastline ahead comes into view as you descend gently to Petard Point **52** (*see map on page 121*). From here you can see Scarborough Castle and your final destination – Filey Brigg.

Caution is needed as you descend to sea level down steep steps **G** through trees to reach the delightful wooded wyke (inlet) of Hayburn Wyke. This wildlife haven is a nature reserve managed by the Yorkshire Wildlife Trust. Cross the footbridge over Hayburn Beck. (A short detour off the path to the left takes you to a delightful small waterfall; well worth a few yards' walk.) Walk uphill through the trees, taking the first left at the footpath junction. You may feel that you deserve a rest at the viewing seat halfway up the hill. At the next junction of paths, turn uphill at 11 o'clock to emerge from the woodland on to level farmland at the top. The coastal path is easily followed to the next inlet (Cloughton Wyke).

The Trail continues round Cloughton Wyke **H**. It then climbs up via steps to the sheer cliff edge of Hundale Point with the rocks of Hundale Scar exposed below high water (*see map on page 123*).

You leave the North York Moors National Park on its southern boundary as you approach the Coastguard Lookout Station **I**. The walking is easy and the route is obvious all the way to Scalby Mills. At Crook Ness **J** you cross a concrete pathway leading down to the beach. The view of some of Scarborough's features – the headland, castle and war memorial on Oliver's Mount – start to become familiar.

Above Scalby Ness Sands **K** there is a footpath leading off the Cleveland Way which provides a good route to the Scarborough youth hostel (turn left at the main road) and a large caravan/camp site (turn right at the main road).

On reaching Scalby Beck **L** continue along its gorse-covered slopes on the seaward side. From the headland above Scalby Mills you have your best view of Scarborough's North Bay. Descend the steps and cross the footbridge over Scalby Beck, turn left, and follow the North Bay Promenade to reach the northern end of Scarborough **53**.

It is possible to complete a circular route, back to Helmsley, by leaving the Cleveland Way at point **K** above Scalby Ness Sands, just to the north of Scarborough. A book on the route, entitled *The Link Through The Tabular Hills Walk*, is published by the North York Moors National Park Authority. The route is 48 miles (77 km) long and passes through farmland, moor and forest, close to the southern boundary of the National Park.

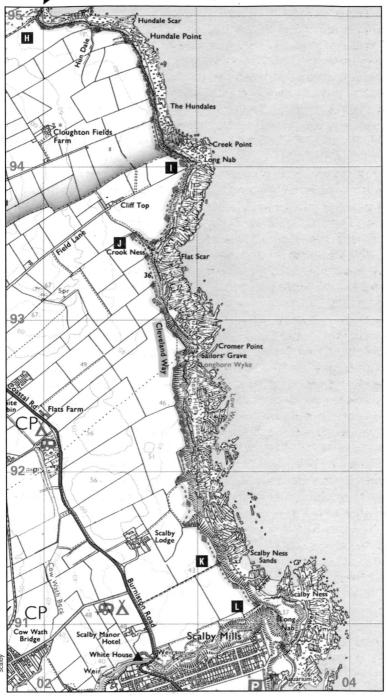

H

Hundale Scar
Hundale Point

The Hundales

Cloughton Fields
Farm

Creek Point
Long Nab

I

Cliff Top

Field Lane

J

Crook Ness

Flat Scar

36

Spr

67

67

60

Cleveland Way

Cromer Point
Sailors' Grave
Longhorn Wyke

49

Coastal Rd

White
Cabin

Flats Farm

46

Mean High Water

Mean Low Water

CP

56

51

40

56

50

Scalby
Lodge

Scalby Ness
Sands

K

43

Scalby Ness

Cow Wath Beck

Burniston Road

CP

48

49

Long
Nab

37

L

Cow Wath
Bridge

Scalby Manor
Hotel

White House

Weir

Scalby Mills

Weir

P

Aquarium

Scalby

02

03

04

95

94

93

92

91

Contours are given in metres
The vertical interval is 10m

123

A CIRCULAR WALK BETWEEN ROBIN HOOD'S BAY AND RAVENSCAR

8 miles (13 km)

This walk follows the coast from Robin Hood's Bay to Ravenscar and returns via an old railway line.

Start at the large car park which occupies the site of the old railway station at Robin Hood's Bay. Walk down through the village to the sea front and follow the route of the Cleveland Way to Ravenscar (see pages 118–120 for route description).

The Cleveland Way meets the railway track-bed on the approach into Ravenscar where there is a wide vehicle track laid with bricks. Return to Robin Hood's Bay along this track-bed when you have visited the village (see page 126). On reaching the tarmac road into Robin Hood's Bay, cross straight over the road and up the track leading into the car park.

Geology of Robin Hood's Bay

Access to a wide wave-cut platform, cliff line exposures with rich fossil beds, quarry face, headland and fault line have all made the Robin Hood's Bay area a place of pilgrimage for those intent on a study of geology. The Ravenscar Trail guidebook, published by the North York Moors National Park, provides an excellent account of the points of interest. All the beds of rock which make up the Middle Jurassic are exhibited between beach level and the top of the Ravenscar quarry.

From a viewpoint halfway down the cliff on the Ravenscar trail, low tide reveals some lessons in geology. A wide wave-cut platform stretches out into the bay. Harder, more resistant layers of rock have produced concentric circles of small ledges (known locally as scars). This is all that is left of the original dome-shaped landform centred out in the bay and subsequently eroded by the action of the sea. Standing on the rocky platform are large isolated blocks of stone. These massive boulders, known as glacial erratics, have stood here for over 10,000 years. Looking straight down on to the shore is a geological fault line which can be seen running seaward from the cliff base. The fault line runs alongside the path, on one side of which are the massive sandstones of the Lower Deltaic period which have clearly been displaced several hundred feet from their original position high on the face of the Ravenscar quarry.

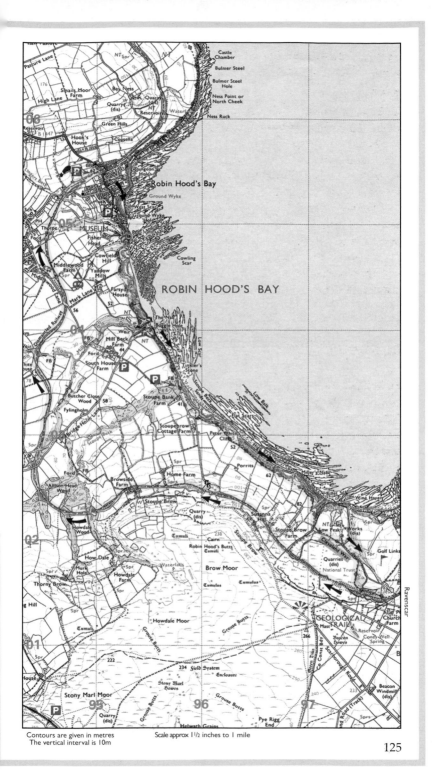

Contours are given in metres
The vertical interval is 10m

Scale approx 1½ inches to 1 mile

Remains of the proposed street layouts for Ravenscar.

Ravenscar

Ravenscar **51** lies at the extreme southern end of Robin Hood's Bay with one of the most beautiful coastal views in Yorkshire. The 600-foot (183-metre) high clifftop village provides a fine vantage point from which to view the 3-mile (5-km) sweep of the bay. On a fine summer's day you could sympathise with the enthusiasm of the developers who, in 1895, purchased the estate and dreamt of building a seaside resort to rival Whitby and Scarborough. The outcome of the venture is obvious as you sense the air of desolation as you walk south out of the village along the Cleveland Way. Roads and sewers were laid, some plots sold and a few villas built but the scheme did not prosper and Ravenscar became 'a town that never was'. In 1913 the development company went bankrupt and the only remnant of its aspirations which has remained commercially viable is the excellent Raven Hall Hotel.

Ravenscar's coastline is now protected through the ownership of the National Trust. Solitude prevails and the view remains. All else in Ravenscar is history – the alum quarries, the brickworks and the abandoned railway station on the Scarborough to Whitby line which closed in March 1965.

Steep, cobbled lanes lead to the stone-built cottages of Robin Hood's Bay.

9 Scarborough to Filey

past Cayton Bay
10¼ miles (16.5 km)

The colourful departure from Scarborough's South Cliff sets you on the final short section of the clifftop trail. The haunting view of continuous coastal cliffs is unbroken after Cayton Bay until you approach Filey.

Scarborough's two bays are separated by an impressive headland. The route along their seaward edge is a distance of about 3 miles (5 km). If you arrive in the height of the summer season and wish to save over an hour's walk along the bustling sea front, there is an alternative. Take an open-top bus from the Corner **A** to the Spa **D** and you can still enjoy the atmosphere and the view, although when the town is not crowded this walk makes a splendid seaside saunter. The Royal Albert Drive (along the North Sands) and the Marine Drive (around the headland) take you to the old tollhouse by the East Pier **B**. The stretch alongside the harbour is Sandside as far as the Scarborough Lifeboat Station **C**. The traditional seaside attractions line Foreshore Road (along the South Sands) before you reach The Spa **D**.

Continue along the roadside footpath leading to The Spa which is the town's leading entertainment and conference centre. Keep ahead, past this long line of buildings and a café on your right, on a broad promenade. (A higher-level pathway, past the beach huts, can also be used on the next section.) Follow the seaside route past the open-air swimming pool **E** which is now no longer in use. Take the steps to the concrete pathway with railings on the seaward side. At the end of this pathway you will see the line of large boulders which provided some coastal protection following the collapse of the Holbeck cliff in June 1993. It is estimated that one million tonnes of material were displaced in the landslip which destroyed the Holbeck Hall Hotel. A gravel path skirts the hillside **F** and provides a fine view across the bay towards the harbour and castle headland.

Near the top of the hill, there is a large car park sited above the grassy bank on your right. On reaching scrub woodland, leave the main recreational path and divert into the clump of trees to follow the Cleveland Way, with a tall fence line on the left, and through an archway of blackthorn bushes. The narrow, and sometimes muddy, path continues along the hillside.

Northstead
Manor
Gardens

A

FB

Falls

North Sands

Coffee Pot

Clarence
Gardens

The
Holms

Castle
(rems of)

78

Hall
(rems of)

Remains of
Chapel of Our Lady
on remains of
ROMAN
SIGNAL STATION

Hosp

Sch

Sch

Gambol Stones

B

Old
Harbour

4

LB Sta

Hosp

C

PO

Lib

St Nicholas
Cliff

53

Sta

Mus

Valley Park

Mus

Offices

Coll

Mean High Water

South Sands

Mean Low Water

SCARBOROUGH

D

The Spa

South Bay

South
Cliff
Gardens

Weaponness

South Cliff

Bathing Pool
(disused)

E

Holbeck
Gardens

Hosp

Sch

61

F

War Meml

Resr

FB

155

Mast

Hotel

Industrial
Estate

Wks

B 1427

Oliver's Mount Plantation

Oliver's Mount

82

94

Colleges

Black Rocks

94

Schs

Wheatcroft Cliff

Club House

South Cliff Golf Course

A 165

Wheatcroft

Golf Course

69

G

The
Mere

135

130

H

PG

Cleve

125

FB

Oliver's
Mount
Farm

113

High Deepdale

110

Knox Hill

110

74

115

110

04

05

Contours are given in metres
The vertical interval is 5m

129

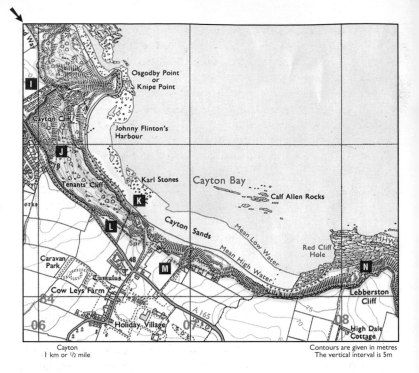

Osgodby Point
or
Knipe Point

Cayton Cliff

Johnny Flinton's
Harbour

Karl Stones

Cayton Bay

Calf Allen Rocks

Tenants' Cliff

Cayton Sands

Mean Low Water

Red Cliff
Hole

Mean High Water

Caravan
Park

Cumulus

Cow Leys Farm

Lebberston
Cliff

Holiday Village

High Dale
Cottage

Cayton
1 km or 1/2 mile

Contours are given in metres
The vertical interval is 5m

Once you have brushed your way through the scrubland which covers this patch of coastal cliff, you emerge on to the clifftop path. The Cleveland Way skirts the edge of the golf course around Wheatcroft Cliff and the headland of White Nab **G**, then descends down steps into a ravine **H**. Turn right up the track, then left at the top through the wood and along the edge of the field.

On reaching the edge of a modern housing development **I**, you turn immediately left down the path and round into the woods of Knipe Point, owned by the National Trust.

The route through the woodland should now be followed carefully. Descend a short way into the wood and immediately take the right fork, continuing downhill and twisting round the bank. Turn right again at the next footpath leading off the main track down a line of wooden steps. At the T-junction with a main track, turn right. After a short distance, turn right along a narrow path off the main track. Cross straight over the stoned path **J** leading down from Osgodby to Johnny Flinton's Harbour. Having navigated your way through this tricky section, you soon emerge on the cliff land overlooking Cayton Bay.

130

The Trail reaches a fence line **K** where you must turn right and climb steeply uphill. At the top of the hill **L** cross over the stile, turn left and continue along the fence line. The path cuts downhill across the corner of the field to reach a stile. Cross the narrow access road and take the left-hand path uphill to the cliff edge. Continue ahead, passing a cottage on your right. Along this next clifftop section you will see a curiously sited wooden bungalow, fenced off right in the middle of the field. The Trail crosses over a tarmac footpath **M** and up to a rail fence where you join the access lane in front of the houses. Beyond the last dwelling the Trail once again becomes a clifftop path. There are appropriate warnings here to take care because of the sheer cliffs. The cries of the gulls greet you from their cliffsite nests on Lebberston Cliff. As you walk, remember to glance back occasionally along the coast to Scarborough's prominent headland.

Do not take the path **N** leading off to Lebberston but continue ahead down the steps overlooking Gristhorpe Sands. The route leads uphill to a caravan site **O** where you walk along the track in front of the caravans.

The Trail leaves the caravan park **P** and takes you along the cliff top to Cunstone Nab from where you view the last lap of coastline to Filey Brigg. Beyond that is the wide sweep of coastline to the chalk cliffs of Flamborough Head.

From Newbiggin Cliff **Q**, the gently sloping farmland to the south reveals a welcome sight of Filey **54** where a celebration

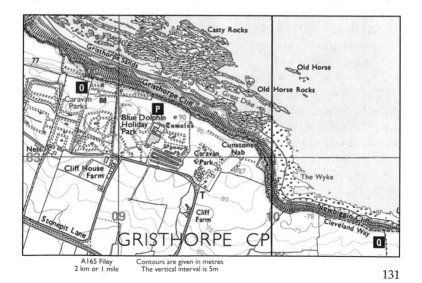

A165 Filey
2 km or 1 mile

Contours are given in metres
The vertical interval is 5m

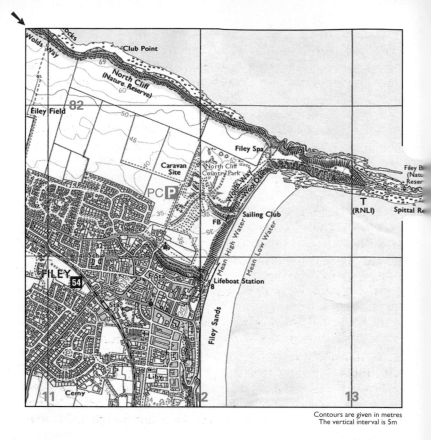

Contours are given in metres
The vertical interval is 5m

of the walk's end will undoubtedly raise morale. The end of one National Trail is the beginning of another – the Wolds Way. This trail offers the perfect extension to the Cleveland Way and a marked contrast in scenery and vegetation. The route, over the Yorkshire Wolds, winds through 79 miles (127 km) of chalk hills and dry valleys to reach Hessle, near Hull, on the banks of the River Humber.

Filey Brigg makes a fine geographical goal as the most easterly point along the whole trail. Take a deep breath of salt sea air at the end of this slender rocky protrusion and savour your position at the edge of the North Sea. If the tide permits, you can walk along the sands into Filey. Alternatively, walk back along the headland (Carr Naze) and then south along the popular clifftop path to reach the sea front at the Coble Landing.

Scarborough

The prominent headland has always been the centrepiece of natural attraction in Scarborough **53** and has been used since Bronze Age times for human settlements, albeit for military purposes. The Romans used it nearly 2,000 years ago for their signal station and the Normans constructed a castle on its easily defended ridge in the 12th century. Facing the North Sea to either side of the castle headland are Scarborough's two sweeping bays with their markedly contrasting developments. The touch-paper which ignited Scarborough's expansion from a Yorkshire fishing town eventually into the premier holiday resort of England's east coast was medicinal spring water. In the early 17th century the curative power of a local spring water turned the town's attention towards visitors. A local doctor acclaimed the beneficial and pleasurable properties of sea-bathing and Scarborough became the country's first seaside resort.

The Victorians fell in love with the resort and the coming of the railway in 1845 ensured easy access for thousands of holiday makers. They lavished style and enthusiasm on the town with the building of the Spa, promenade, fine houses, shops, theatres and landscape gardens. These, coupled with its wide range of modern amusements, ensure that the attribute 'something for everyone' must be as true for Scarborough as for anywhere in the world.

Filey

A fishing community turned holiday resort, Filey **54** is probably best known for its headland and the remarkable slab of calcareous gritstone protruding into the sea – Filey Brigg. The town lies sheltered by the headland at the northern end of a magnificent sweep of coastline with 6 miles (10 km) of sandy beach stretching halfway to Flamborough Head. Filey offers the traditional seaside holiday with all the ingredients of an old fishing quarter enlivened by Victorian embellishments and modern amusements, but in a relatively compact and composed fashion. The flavour of the town and its superb coastal view make a pleasant and practical end to the Cleveland Way.

Scarborough still prospers as a busy harbour port. Its fame and fortune as a seaside resort rose rapidly during the Victorian era.

PART THREE

USEFUL
INFORMATION

Transport

Bus and rail access to and from the Cleveland Way is easy. Rail services connect to York, Malton, Thirsk, Northallerton, Middlesbrough, Saltburn, Great Ayton, Whitby, Scarborough and Filey. For train times, call National Rail Enquiries, tel. 08457 484950.

In addition, bus services can get you to the start of the Cleveland Way at Helmsley from York, Scarborough and Malton. Why not use the Moorsbus Network's very own Cleveland Way Explorer, which connects many of the previously unserved western parts of the National Trail.

Complementing these services are regular bus services that operate to key villages and towns on the Cleveland Way. Telephone Traveline on 0870 608 2608 for both national and local bus information.

Details of all rail and bus services in the North York Moors and East Coast area are published in the *Moors Explorer* booklet, available free from North York Moors National Park Authority and Tourist Information Centres in this area.

Comprehensive travel information for the North York Moors area is also available on the Internet at www.moorsbus.net. Another good source of information is the official National Trail website: www.clevelandway.gov.uk

North Sea Ferries

A bus service connects the ferry terminal at Hull with the rail and bus stations in Hull. Moorsbus services operate from here during the summer.

Car parking in Helmsley

If you intend to drive to Helmsley and to park your car in the town for a week or more you should contact the Police Station, Ashdale Road, Helmsley, York YO62 5DB. Either post or deliver a list of the following details to them: (1) name; (2) home address and telephone number; (3) make of car; (4) registration number; (5) parking location; (6) date of departure from Helmsley; (7) date of return to Helmsley. Helmsley Police Station is not open on a regular basis. You can contact the Malton Police Station (tel. 01653 692424).

There is a car park on the north side of the town at the start of the Cleveland Way and a weekly parking ticket is available from the Helmsley Tourist Information Centre in the Market Place. You will be able to return to Helmsley by bus from Filey via Scarborough.

Accommodation

Bed and breakfast
Your schedule will be dictated largely by the availability of accommodation. This is relatively plentiful along the east coast, but is somewhat restricted on the inland section along the edge of the Cleveland Hills.

A *Cleveland Way Accommodation and Information Guide* is published annually. It is available from the Cleveland Way Project Officer, North York Moors National Park Authority, The Old Vicarage, Bondgate, Helmsley, York YO62 5BP. In addition, Tourist Information Centres in the area may be able to assist if you meet with particular problems (*see page 139*). Information on accommodation can also be found in *Stilwell's National Trail Companion*, which is published annually.

The following list of places which usually offer accommodation will be useful in planning your programme. In some cases the actual location may be a short distance away from the Cleveland Way and not shown on the map in this guidebook.

Accommodation places

Helmsley
Scawton
Old Byland
Cold Kirby
Sutton Bank
Kilburn
Boltby
Over Silton
Osmotherley
Ingleby Cross
Faceby
Carlton in Cleveland
Carlton Bank
Staithes
Port Mulgrave

Kirby in Cleveland
Clay Bank
Chopgate
Great Broughton
Ingleby Greenhow
Kildale
Great Ayton
Guisborough
Slapewath
Skelton
Saltburn
Skinningrove
Loftus
Robin Hood's Bay
Ravenscar

Runswick Bay
Mickleby
Kettleness
Sandsend
Whitby
High Hawsker

Staintondale
Hayburn Wyke
Cloughton
Scarborough
Filey

Youth hostels
Youth hostels offer low-cost accommodation for people of all ages and many hostels provide a full catering service. There are five hostels along the route of the Cleveland Way; their locations are marked on the maps.

Helmsley Youth Hostel, tel. 01439 770433
Osmotherley Youth Hostel, tel. 01609 883575
Whitby Youth Hostel, tel. 01947 602878
Boggle Hole Youth Hostel, tel. 01947 880352
Scarborough Youth Hostel, tel. 01723 361176

Details of Youth Hostels Association (YHA) membership and all the above hostels are available from YHA, Trevelyan House, Dimple Road, Matlock, Derbyshire DE4 3XA. Tel. 0870 870 8808.

Camping
Details of camp sites are included in the *Cleveland Way Accommodation and Information Guide*, available from the Cleveland Way Project Officer (*see page 137*). In addition to the listed camp sites, many farmers are willing to allow camping on the basis of a personal enquiry. Such sites offer no facilities other than a pitch and water supply and are intended for use as overnight stops only. All camping requires the permission of the landowner or farmer. Please remember that camping on the open moorland and in the forest is not permitted due to the risk of fire.

Information Centres

The official Tourist Information Centres (TICs) are useful sources of information concerning accommodation, camping, public transport and local services. There are six TICs along the Cleveland Way at Helmsley, Sutton Bank, Saltburn, Whitby, Scarborough and Filey. The following list includes a number of additional TICs, in case you arrive at these locations by public transport. There is also a National Trust Centre at Ravenscar. Many of them are open in the summer only.

Filey TIC, John Street, Filey, YO14 9DW. Tel. 01723 518000.

Great Ayton TIC, High Green Car Park, Great Ayton, TS9 6BJ. Tel. 01642 722835.

Guisborough TIC, Priory Grounds, Church Street, Guisborough TS14 6HG. Tel. 01287 633801.

Helmsley TIC, Town Hall, Market Place, Helmsley, North Yorkshire YO62 5BL. Tel. 01439 770173.

Malton TIC, 58 Market Place, Malton YO17 7LW. Tel. 01653 600048.

Middlesbrough TIC, 99–101 Albert Road, Middlesbrough TS1 2PA. Tel. 01642 243425.

Pickering TIC, The Ropery, Pickering YO18 8DY. Tel. 01751 473791.

Ravenscar National Trust Centre, Ravenscar, Scarborough YO13 0NE. Tel. 01723 870138.

Saltburn TIC, 3 Station Buildings, Station Square, Saltburn TS12 1AQ. Tel. 01287 622422.

Scarborough TIC, Unit 3, Pavilion House, Valley Bridge Road, Scarborough YO11 1UZ. Tel. 01723 373333.

Sutton Bank National Park Visitor Centre, Sutton Bank, Thirsk YO7 2EH. Tel. 01845 597426.

Thirsk TIC, 23 Kirkgate, Thirsk YO7 1PL. Tel. 01845 522755.

Whitby TIC, Langborne Road, Whitby YO21 1YN. Tel. 01947 602674.

York TIC, De Grey Rooms, Exhibition Square, York YO1 2HB. Tel. 01904 621756.

Equipment

There is a bewildering range of choice when it comes to selecting footwear and clothing. There are, however, a few comments worth bearing in mind. Lightweight walking boots are recommended in preference to walking shoes for the Cleveland Way. The main disadvantage of walking shoes is that they do not provide any ankle support. Apart from the distance involved in your daily target, there are a number of sections along the moor and coast where the ankle support provided by boots will greatly ease your walking. Do consider selecting a size of boot which allows for two pairs of socks – one thin (inner pair), one thick (outer pair). Two layers of socks cushion the feet, absorb a lot of friction and reduce the chance of blisters.

It is unlikely that you will complete the Cleveland Way without experiencing some wind and rain. The chilling effect of wind requires some windproof clothing; waterproofs are needed to combat the rain. Nylon proofed garments may provide total sealing but this inevitably means no ventilation, and condensation results in clammy discomfort. The more expensive breathable waterproofed garments greatly assist in overcoming this problem. We tend to judge our requirement for clothing according to the season and the prevailing weather conditions. Unfortunately the first is an unreliable guide and the second offers no guarantee for the day in question. You should be prepared for rain and within a day's walking you should anticipate being both too hot and too cold: even in summer the moors can be cold. An extra pullover, gloves, headgear and waterproofs are the main 'extras' in case of sudden changes in the weather. Make sure that you have adequate food and liquid refreshment for a day's walk.

Emergency equipment

The following items are recommended as emergency equipment: compass, torch, whistle, first-aid kit, food rations and survival bag. In weather conditions of failing visibility a compass may be a necessity. The torch or whistle can be used to give the International Distress Signal. In case of minor injuries it is a wise policy to carry a small first-aid kit. Emergency food rations, such as glucose sweets, barley sugar, chocolate, mint cake and dried fruit, will provide you with much-needed energy. If you are intent on a fairly high mileage target each day you should consider carrying a polythene survival bag in case you are forced to spend a night in the open.

Local facilities

Some local facilities of interest to walkers are listed below, and some will also be marked on the map. Unfortunately many facilities in rural areas face an uncertain future and inclusion on this list today is no guarantee for tomorrow. You will not have any difficulty in obtaining information on local facilities wherever there is a tourist information centre (TIC) – either in person or by telephone. Details are also given in the *Cleveland Way Accommodation and Information Guide* available from the Cleveland Way Project Officer (*see page 137*).

Helmsley: bus, café, PO, pub, shop, tel, TIC, wc
Rievaulx: tel, wc
Cold Kirby: PO, tel
Hambleton: pub
Sutton Bank: café, tel, TIC, wc
Osmotherley: bus, café, PO, pub, shop, tel, wc
Husthwaite Green: tel
Carlton Park: café
Clay Bank: bus
Kildale: café, PO, rail, tel
Slapewarth: bus, pub
Skelton Green: bus, PO, pub
Skelton: bus, café, PO, pub, shop, tel, wc
Saltburn: all facilities
Skinningrove: bus, PO, pub, shop, tel, wc
Boulby: bus
Staithes: bus, café, PO, pub, tel, wc
Port Mulgrave: pub, tel
Runswick Bay: bus, pub, tel, wc
Goldsborough: pub
Sandsend: bus, café, PO, pub, shop, tel, wc
Whitby: all facilities
Robin Hood's Bay: bus, café, PO, pub, shop, tel, wc
Ravenscar: bus, café, PO, pub, shop, tel, wc
Scarborough: all facilities
Filey: all facilities

All facilities: bus=bus service stop; café; PO=post office; pub=public house; rail=railway station; shop; tel=public telephone; TIC=Tourist Information Centre; wc=public toilets.

Early closing and market days

Many shops dispense with early closing during the summer months. Market days are colourful local events and will provide an interesting browse if you have the time.

	early closing	market day
Helmsley	Wed	Fri
Guisborough	Wed	Thurs
Saltburn	Tues	—
Whitby	Wed	Mon, Wed
Scarborough	Wed	Thurs
Filey	Wed	—

Useful addresses and telephone numbers

North York Moors National Park Authority, The Old Vicarage, Bondgate, Helmsley, York YO62 5BP. Tel. 01439 770657 (for literature, accommodation and route enquiries). E-mail: info@northyorkmoors-npa.gov.uk

Redcar & Cleveland Borough Council, Town Hall, Fabian Road, South Bank, Middlesbrough TS6 9AR. Tel: 01642 444000.

Scarborough Borough Council, Town Hall, St Nicholas Street, Scarborough YO11 2HG. Tel: 01723 232323.

Heritage Coast Ranger, The Moors Centre, Danby, Whitby YO21 2NB. Tel: 01287 660340 (for Heritage Coast literature, guided walks programme and route enquiries).

Countryside Agency (Headquarters), John Dower House, Crescent Place, Cheltenham GL50 3RA. Tel: 01242 521381 (for literature on all National Trails).

Countryside Agency, Yorkshire & the Humber Regional Office, 4th Floor, Victoria Wharf Embankment IV, Sovereign Street, Leeds LS1 4BA. Tel: 0113 246 9222 (for literature on National Trails and other walks in the region).

National Trust, Yorkshire Region, Goddards, 27 Tadcaster Road, Dringhouses, York YO24 1GG. Tel: 01904 702021 (for information on membership and properties).

Bibliography

The North York Moors National Park Authority publishes a wide range of leaflets, booklets and books on the moors and a list is available on request. Information centres and local bookshops stock a range of published material on the North York Moors.

Cleveland Way guidebooks

Boyes, Malcolm, *A Guide to the Cleveland Way and Missing Link* (Constable, 1977).

Collins, Martin, *Cleveland Way plus the Tabular Hills Link* (Dalesman Books, 1997).

Hannon, Paul, *Cleveland Way Companion* (Hillside Publications, 1992).

Sale, Richard, *A Guide to the Cleveland Way* (Constable, 1987).

The Cleveland Way (Footprint, 1992).

General guidebooks

Osborne, Roger and Bowden, Alastair, *The Dinosaur Coast: Yorkshire Rocks, Reptiles and Landscapes* (North York Moors National Park Authority, 2001).

Sampson, Ian, *The Official Guidebook to the North York Moors National Park* (Pevensey Guides, 2001).

Spratt and Harrison (eds), *Landscape Heritage of the North York Moors* (North York Moors National Park Authority, 1989).

Sykes, Nan, *Wild Plants and their Habitats in the North York Moors* (North York Moors National Park Authority, 1993).

The North York Moors (Insight Guides, 1999).

The North York Moors (Pathfinder Guides, Jarrolds, 1998).

Ordnance Leisure Guide to North York Moors (AA/Ordnance Survey, 1996).

Ordnance Survey maps covering the Cleveland Way

Explorer Maps (scale 1:25 000): 301 and 306.

Outdoor Leisure Maps (scale 1:25 000): Map 26 North York Moors – West; Map 27 North York Moors – East.

Motoring Maps: Reach the Cleveland Way using Travelmaster Maps 5, 'Northern England', and 6, 'East Midlands and Yorkshire' (scale 1:250 000).

Any comments concerning the Cleveland Way should be sent to the Cleveland Way Project Officer, North York Moors National Park Authority, The Old Vicarage, Bondgate, Helmsley, York YO62 5BP.